The Massey Lectures Series

The Massey Lectures are co-sponsored by CBC Radio, House of Anansi Press, and Massey College, in the University of Toronto. The series was created in honour of the Right Honourable Vincent Massey, former governor general of Canada, and was inaugurated in 1961 to provide a forum on radio where major contemporary thinkers could address important issues of our time.

This book comprises the 2003 Massey Lectures, "The Truth About Stories," broadcast in November 2003 as part of CBC Radio's *Ideas* series. The producer of the series was Philip Coulter; the executive producer was Bernie Lucht.

Thomas King

Thomas King holds a Ph.D. in English/American Studies from the University of Utah and has taught Native Studies in Utah, Minnesota, and Alberta for the past twenty-five years. He is currently Professor of English (teaching Native Literature and Creative Writing) at the University of Guelph. His widely acclaimed novels include *Medicine River*, *Green Grass, Running Water*, and *Truth and Bright Water*, and he has been nominated for the Governor General's Award as well as the Commonwealth Writers' Prize. King has also written the short-story collection *A Short History of Indians in Canada*. He is the editor of *All My Relations: An Anthology of Contemporary Canadian Native Fiction*, and co-editor of *The Native in Literature: Canadian and Comparative Perspectives*. He is also known for his popular CBC Radio series, *The Dead Dog Café Comedy Hour*, which aired from 1997 to 2000, and in 2002 and 2006. His father was Cherokee, his mother is Greek, and King is the first Massey lecturer of Native descent.

D0029085

ALSO BY THOMAS KING

FICTION
Medicine River
Green Grass, Running Water
One Good Story, That One
Truth and Bright Water
A Short History of Indians in Canada

FOR CHILDREN
A Coyote Columbus Story
Coyote Sings to the Moon
Coyote's New Suit
A Coyote Solstice Tale

AS EDITOR
All My Relations: An Anthology of Contemporary Canadian Native Fiction
The Native in Literature: Canadian and Comparative Perspectives
First Voices, First Words

THE TRUTH ABOUT STORIES

A Native Narrative

THOMAS KING

ANANSI

Copyright © 2003 Dead Dog Café Productions Inc. and
the Canadian Broadcasting Corporation

All rights reserved. No part of this publication may be
reproduced or transmitted in any form or by any means,
electronic or mechanical, including photocopying, recording,
or any information storage and retrieval system, without
permission in writing from the publisher.

Published in 2003 by
House of Anansi Press Inc.
110 Spadina Avenue, Suite 801
Toronto, ON, M5V 2K4
Tel. 416-363-4343
Fax 416-363-1017
www.houseofanansi.com

Distributed in Canada by
HarperCollins Canada Ltd.
1995 Markham Road
Scarborough, ON, M1B 5M8
Toll free tel. 1-800-387-0117

CBC and Massey College logos used with permission

The publisher gratefully acknowledges kind permission
to reprint excerpts from the following:

(pp. 44, 93, and 95) *I Hear the Train: Reflections, Inventions, Refractions* by
Louis Owens, © 2001 University of Oklahoma Press. Used by permission.
(p. 62) "The Halfbreed Blues" by Andrea Menard,
words and music © 2000 Andrea Menard, SOCAN. Used by permission.

House of Anansi Press is committed to protecting our natural environment. As part of our efforts,
the interior of this book is printed on paper that contains 100% post-consumer recycled fibres, is
acid-free, and is processed chlorine-free.

17 16 15 14 13   12 13 14 15 16

LIBRARY AND ARCHIVES CANADA CATALOGUING IN PUBLICATION DATA

King, Thomas, 1943–
The truth about stories : a native narrative / Thomas King.

(CBC Massey lectures series)
ISBN 978-0-88784-696-0

I. Title. II. Series.

PS8571.I5298T77 2003   C813'.54   C2003-904921-3

Cover design: Bill Douglas
Cover photo: Thomas King
Typesetting: Brian Panhuyzen

 Canada Council   Conseil des Arts   ONTARIO ARTS COUNCIL
for the Arts   du Canada   CONSEIL DES ARTS DE L'ONTARIO

*We acknowledge for their financial support of our publishing program
the Canada Council for the Arts, the Ontario Arts Council, and the Government of Canada
through the Canada Book Fund.*

Printed and bound in Canada

MIX
Paper from
responsible sources
FSC
www.fsc.org   FSC® C004071

ANCIENT FOREST ™
FRIENDLY

For Helen, who has heard these stories before

Contents

I

"YOU'LL NEVER BELIEVE WHAT HAPPENED" IS ALWAYS A GREAT WAY TO START

THERE IS A STORY I KNOW. It's about the earth and how it floats in space on the back of a turtle. I've heard this story many times, and each time someone tells the story, it changes. Sometimes the change is simply in the voice of the storyteller. Sometimes the change is in the details. Sometimes in the order of events. Other times it's the dialogue or the response of the audience. But in all the tellings of all the tellers, the world never leaves the turtle's back. And the turtle never swims away.

One time, it was in Prince Rupert I think, a young girl in the audience asked about the turtle and the earth. If the earth was on the back of a turtle, what was below the turtle? Another turtle, the storyteller told her. And below that turtle? Another turtle. And below that? Another turtle.

The girl began to laugh, enjoying the game, I imagine. So how many turtles are there? she wanted to know. The storyteller shrugged. No one knows for sure, he told her, but it's turtles all the way down.

The truth about stories is that that's all we are. The Okanagan storyteller Jeannette Armstrong tells us that "Through my language I understand I am being spoken to, I'm not the one speaking. The words are coming from many tongues and mouths of Okanagan people and the land around them. I am a listener to the language's stories, and when my words form I am merely retelling the same stories in different patterns."[1]

When I was a kid, I was partial to stories about other worlds and interplanetary travel. I used to imagine that I could just gaze off into space and be whisked to another planet, much like John Carter in Edgar Rice Burroughs's Mars series. I'd like to tell you that I was interested in outer space or that the stars fascinated me or that I was curious about the shape and nature of the universe. Fact of the matter was I just wanted to get out of town. Wanted to get as far away from where I was as I could. At fifteen, Pluto looked good. Tiny, cold, lonely. As far from the sun as you could get.

I'm sure part of it was teenage angst, and part of it was being poor in a rich country, and part of it was knowing that white was more than just a colour. And part of it was seeing the world through my mother's eyes.

My mother raised my brother and me by herself, in an era when women were not welcome in the workforce, when their proper place was out of sight in the home. It was supposed to be a luxury granted women by men. But having misplaced her man, or more properly having had him misplace himself, she had no such luxury and was caught between what she was supposed to be — invisible and female — and what circumstances dictated she become — visible and, well, not male. Self-supporting perhaps. That was it. Visible and self-supporting.

As a child and as a young man, I watched her make her way from doing hair in a converted garage to designing tools for the aerospace industry. It was a long, slow journey. At Aerojet in California, she began as a filing clerk. By the end of the first year, she was doing drafting work, though she was still classified and paid as a filing clerk. By the end of the second year, with night school stuffed into the cracks, she was doing numerical-control engineering and was still classified and paid as a filing clerk.

It was, after all, a man's world, and each step she took had to be made as quietly as possible, each movement camouflaged against complaint. For over thirty years, she held to the shadows, stayed in the shade.

I knew the men she worked with. They were our neighbours and our friends. I listened to their stories about work and play, about their dreams and their disappointments. Your mother, they liked to tell me, is just one of the boys. But she wasn't. I knew it. She knew it better.

In 1963, my mother and five of her colleagues were recruited by the Boeing Company to come to Seattle, Washington, as part of a numerical-control team. Everyone was promised equal status, which, for my mother, meant being brought into Boeing as a fully fledged, salaried engineer.

So she went. It was more money, more prestige. And when she got there, she was told that, while everyone else would be salaried and would have engineer status, she would be an hourly employee and would have the same status as the other two women in the department, who were production assistants. So after selling everything in order to make the move, she found herself in a job where she made considerably less than the other members of the team, where she had to punch a time clock, and where she wasn't even eligible for benefits or a pension.

She objected. That wasn't the promise, she told her supervisor. You brought everyone else in as equals, why not me?

She didn't really have to ask that question. She knew the answer. You probably know it, too. The other five members of the team were men. She was the only woman. Don't worry, she was told, if your work is good, you'll get promoted at the end of the first year.

So she waited. There wasn't much she could do about it. And at the end of the first year, when the review of her work came back satisfactory, she was told she would have to wait another year. And when that year was up . . .

I told her she was crazy to allow people to treat her like that. But she knew the nature of the world in which she lived, and I did not. And yet she has lived her life with an optimism of the intellect and an optimism of the will. She understands the world as a good place where good deeds should beget good rewards. At eighty-one, she still believes that that world is possible, even though she will now admit she never found it, never even caught a glimpse of it.

My father is a different story. I didn't know him. He left when I was three or four. I have one memory of a man who took me to a small café that had wooden booths with high backs and a green parrot that pulled at my hair. I don't think this was my father. But it might have been.

For a long time I told my friends that my father had died, which was easier than explaining that he had left us. Then when I was nine, I think, my mother got a call from him asking if he could come home and start over. My mother said okay. I'll be home in three days, he told her.

And that was the last we ever heard from him.

My mother was sure that something had happened to him. Somewhere between Chicago and California. No one would call to say they were coming home and then not show up, unless they had been injured or killed. So she waited for him. So did I.

And then when I was fifty-six or fifty-seven, my brother called me. Sit down, Christopher said, I've got some news. I was living in Ontario, and I figured that if my brother was calling me all the way from California, telling me to sit down, it had to be bad news, something to do with my mother.

But it wasn't.

You'll never believe what happened, my brother said.

That's always a good way to start a story, you know: you'll never believe what happened.

And he was right.

We found our father. That's exactly what he said. We found our father.

I had dreamed about such an occurrence. Finding my father. Not as a child, but as a grown man. One of my more persistent fictions was to catch up with him in a bar, sitting on a stool, having a beer. A dark, dank bar, stinking of sorrow, a bar where men who had deserted their families went to drink and die.

He wouldn't recognize me. I'd sit next to him, and after a while the two of us would strike up a conversation.

What do you do for a living? How do you like the new Ford? You believe those Blue Jays?

Guy talk. Short sentences. Lots of nodding.

You married? Any kids?

And then I'd give him a good look at me. A good, long look. And just as he began to remember, just as he began to realize who I might be, I'd leave. *Hasta la vista.* Toodle-oo. See you around. I wouldn't tell him about my life or what I had been able to accomplish, or how many grand-children he had or how much I had missed not having a father in my life.

Screw him. I had better things to do than sit around with some old bastard and talk about life and responsibility.

So when my brother called to tell me that we had found our father, I ran through the bar scene one more time. So I'd be ready.

Here's what had happened. My father had two sisters. We didn't know them very well, and, when my father disappeared, we lost track of that side of the family. So we had no way of knowing that when my father left us, he vanished from his sisters' lives as well. I suppose they thought he was dead, too. But evidently his oldest sister wasn't sure, and, after she had retired and was getting on in years, she decided to make one last attempt to find out what had happened to him.

She was not a rich woman, but she spotted an advertisement in a local newspaper that offered the services of a detective who would find lost or missing relatives for $75. Flat rate. Satisfaction guaranteed.

My brother took a long time in telling this story, drawing out the details, repeating the good parts, making me wait.

The detective, it turned out, was a retired railroad employee who knew how to use a computer and a phone book. If Robert King was alive and if he hadn't changed his name, he'd have a phone and an address. If he was dead, there should be a death certificate floating around somewhere. The detective's name was Fred or George, I don't remember, and he was a bulldog.

It took him two days. Robert King was alive and well, in Illinois.

Christopher stopped at this point in the story to let me catch my breath. I was already making reservations to fly to Chicago, to rent a car, to find that bar.

That's the good news, my brother told me.

One of the tricks to storytelling is, never to tell everything at once, to make your audience wait, to keep everyone in suspense.

My father had married two more times. Christopher

had all the details. Seven other children. Seven brothers and sisters we had never known about. Barbara, Robert, Kelly.

What's the bad news? I wanted to know.

Oh, that, said my brother. The bad news is he's dead.

Evidently, just after the railroad detective found him, my father slipped in a river, hit his head on a rock, and died in a hospital. My aunt, the one who had hired the detective, went to Illinois for the funeral and to meet her brother's other families for the first time.

You're going to like the next part, my brother told me.

I should warn you that my brother has a particular fondness for irony.

When my aunt got to the funeral, the oldest boy, Robert King Jr., evidently began a sentence with "I guess as the oldest boy . . ." Whereupon my aunt told the family about Christopher and me.

They knew about each other. The two families. Were actually close, but they had never heard about us. My father had never mentioned us. It was as though he had disposed of us somewhere along the way, dropped us in a trash can by the side of the road.

That's my family. These are their stories.

So what? I've heard worse stories. So have you. Open today's paper and you'll find two or three that make mine sound like a Disney trailer. Starvation. Land mines. Suicide bombings. Sectarian violence. Sexual abuse. Children stacked up like cordwood in refugee camps around the globe. So what makes my mother's sacrifice special? What makes my father's desertion unusual?

Absolutely nothing.

Matter of fact, the only people who have any interest in either of these stories are my brother and me. I tell the stories not to play on your sympathies but to suggest how stories can control our lives, for there is a part of me that has never been able to move past these stories, a part of me that will be chained to these stories as long as I live.

Stories are wondrous things. And they are dangerous. The Native novelist Leslie Silko, in her book *Ceremony*, tells how evil came into the world. It was witch people. Not Whites or Indians or Blacks or Asians or Hispanics. Witch people. Witch people from all over the world, way back when, and they all came together for a witches' conference. In a cave. Having a good time. A contest, actually. To see who could come up with the scariest thing. Some of them brewed up potions in pots. Some of them jumped in and out of animal skins. Some of them thought up charms and spells.

It must have been fun to watch.

Until finally there was only one witch left who hadn't done anything. No one knew where this witch came from or if the witch was male or female. And all this witch had was a story.

Unfortunately the story this witch told was an awful thing full of fear and slaughter, disease and blood. A story of murderous mischief. And when the telling was done, the other witches quickly agreed that this witch had won the prize.

"Okay you win," they said. "[B]ut what you said just now — it isn't so funny. It doesn't sound so good. We are doing okay without it. We can get along without that kind of thing. Take it back. Call that story back."[2]

But, of course, it was too late. For once a story is told, it cannot be called back. Once told, it is loose in the world.

So you have to be careful with the stories you tell. And you have to watch out for the stories that you are told. But if I ever get to Pluto, that's how I would like to begin. With a story. Maybe I'd tell the inhabitants of Pluto one of the stories I know. Maybe they'd tell me one of theirs. It wouldn't matter who went first. But which story? That's the real question. Personally, I'd want to hear a creation story, a story that recounts how the world was formed, how things came to be, for contained within creation stories are relationships that help to define the nature of the universe and how cultures understand the world in which they exist.

And, as luck would have it, I happen to know a few. But I have a favourite. It's about a woman who fell from the sky. And it goes like this.

Back at the beginning of imagination, the world we know as earth was nothing but water, while above the earth, somewhere in space, was a larger, more ancient world. And on that world was a woman.

A crazy woman.

Well, she wasn't exactly crazy. She was more nosy. Curious. The kind of curious that doesn't give up. The kind that follows you around. Now, we all know that being curious is healthy, but being *curious* can get you into trouble.

Don't be too curious, the Birds told her.

Okay, she said, I won't.

But you know what? That's right. She kept on being curious.

One day while she was bathing in the river, she happened to look at her feet and discovered that she had five toes on each foot. One big one and four smaller ones. They had been there all along, of course, but now that the woman noticed them for the first time, she wondered why she had five toes instead of three. Or eight. And she wondered if more toes were better than fewer toes.

So she asked her Toes. Hey, she said, how come there are only five of you?

You're being curious again, said her Toes.

Another day, the woman was walking through the forest and found a moose relaxing in the shade by a lake.

Hello, said the Moose. Aren't you that nosy woman?

Yes, I am, said the woman, and what I want to know is why you are so much larger than me.

That's easy, said the Moose, and he walked into the lake and disappeared.

Don't you love cryptic stories? I certainly do.

Now before we go any further, we should give this woman a name so we don't have to keep calling her "the woman." How about Blanche? Catherine? Thelma? Okay, I know expressing an opinion can be embarrassing. So let's do it the way we always do it and let someone else make the decision for us. Someone we trust. Someone who will promise to lower taxes. Someone like me.

I say we call her Charm. Don't worry. We can change it later on if we want to.

So one day the woman we've decided to call Charm went looking for something good to eat. She looked at the fish, but she was not in the mood for fish. She looked at the rabbit, but she didn't feel like eating rabbit either.

I've got this craving, said Charm.

What kind of craving? said Fish.

I want to eat something, but I don't know what it is.

Maybe you're pregnant, said Rabbit. Whenever I get pregnant, I get cravings.

Hmmmm, said Charm, maybe I am.

And you know what? She was.

What you need, Fish and Rabbit told Charm, is some Red Fern Foot.

Yes, said Charm, that sounds delicious. What is it?

It's a root, said Fish, and it only grows under the oldest trees. And it's the perfect thing for pregnant humans.

Now, you're probably thinking that this is getting pretty silly, what with chatty fish and friendly rabbits, with moose disappearing into lakes and talking toes. And you're probably wondering how in the world I expect you to believe any of this, given the fact that we live in a predominantly scientific, capitalistic, Judeo-Christian world governed by physical laws, economic imperatives, and spiritual precepts.

Is that what you're thinking?

It's okay. You won't hurt my feelings.

So Charm went looking for some Red Fern Foot. She dug around this tree and she dug around that tree, but she couldn't find any. Finally she came to the oldest tree in the forest and she began digging around its base. By now she was very hungry, and she was very keen on some Red Fern Foot, so she really got into the digging. And before long she had dug a rather deep hole.

Don't dig too deep, Badger told her.

Mind your own business, Charm told him.

Okay, said Badger, but don't blame me if you make a mistake.

You can probably guess what happened. That's right, Charm dug right through to the other side of the world.

That's curious, said Charm, and she stuck her head into that hole so she could get a better view.

That's very curious, she said again, and she stuck her head even farther into the hole.

Sometimes when I tell this story to children, I slow it down and have Charm stick her head into that hole by degrees. But most of you are adults and have already figured out that Charm is going to stick her head into that hole so far that she's either going to get stuck or she's going to fall through.

And sure enough, she fell through. Right through that hole and into the sky.

Uh-oh, Charm thought to herself. That wasn't too smart.

But she couldn't do much about it now. And she began to tumble through the sky, began to fall and fall and fall and fall. Spinning and turning, floating through the vast expanse of space.

And off in the distance, just on the edge of sight, was a small blue dot floating in the heavens. And as Charm tumbled down through the black sky, the dot got bigger and bigger.

You've probably figured this part out, too, but just so there's no question, this blue dot is the earth. Well, sort of. It's the earth when it was young. When there was nothing but water. When it was simply a water world.

And Charm was heading right for it.

In the meantime, on this water world, on earth, a bunch of water animals were swimming and floating around and diving and talking about how much fun water is.

Water, water, water, said the Ducks. There's nothing like water.

Yes, said the Muskrats, we certainly like being wet.

It's even better when you're under water, said the Sunfish.

Try jumping into it, said the Dolphins. And just as the Dolphins said this, they looked up into the sky.

Uh-oh, said the Dolphins, and everyone looked up in time to see Charm falling toward them. And as she came around the moon, the water animals were suddenly faced with four variables — mass, velocity, compression, and displacement — and with two problems.

The Ducks, who have great eyesight, could see that Charm weighed in at about 150 pounds. And the Beavers, who have a head for physics and math, knew that she was coming in fast. Accelerating at thirty-two feet per second per second to be precise (give or take a little for drag and atmospheric friction). And the Whales knew from many years of study that water does not compress, while the Dolphins could tell anyone who asked that while it won't compress, water will displace.

Which brought the animals to the first of the two problems. If Charm hit the water at full speed, it was going to create one very large tidal wave and ruin everyone's day.

So quick as they could, all the water birds flew up and formed a net with their bodies, and, as Charm came streaking down, the birds caught her, broke her fall, and brought her gently to the surface of the water.

Just in time.

To deal with the second of the two problems. Where to put her.

They could just dump her in the water, but it didn't take a pelican to see that Charm was not a water creature.

Can you swim? asked the Sharks.

Not very well, said Charm.

How about holding your breath for a long time? asked the Sea Horses.

Maybe for a minute or two, said Charm.

Floating? said the Seals. Can you float?

I don't know, said Charm. I never really tried floating.

So what are we going to do with you? said the Lobsters.

Hurry up, said the Birds, flapping their wings as hard as they could.

Perhaps you could put me on something large and flat, Charm told the water animals.

Well, as it turns out, the only place in this water world that was large and flat was the back of the Turtle.

Oh, okay, said Turtle. But if anyone else falls out of the sky, she's on her own.

So the water animals put Charm on the back of the Turtle, and everyone was happy. Well, at least for the next month or so. Until the animals noticed that Charm was going to have a baby.

It's going to get a little crowded, said the Muskrats.

What are we going to do? said the Geese.

It wouldn't be so crowded, Charm told the water animals, if we had some dry land.

Sure, agreed the water animals, even though they had no idea what dry land was.

Charm looked over the side of the Turtle, down into the water, and then she turned to the water animals.

Who's the best diver? she asked.

A contest! screamed the Ducks.

All right! shouted the Muskrats.

What do we have to do? asked the Eels.

It's easy, said Charm. One of you has to dive down to the bottom of the water and bring up some mud.

Sure, said all the water animals, even though they had no idea what mud was.

So, said Charm, who wants to try first?

Me! said Pelican, and he flew into the sky as high as he could and then dropped like a knife into the water. And he was gone for a long time. But when he floated to the surface, out of breath, he didn't have any mud.

It was real dark down there, said Pelican, and cold.

The next animal to try was Walrus.

I don't mind the dark, said Walrus, and my blubber will keep me warm. So down she went, and she was gone for much longer than Pelican, but when she came to the surface coughing up water, she didn't have any mud, either.

I don't think the water has a bottom, said Walrus. Sorry.

I'm sure you're beginning to wonder if there's a point to this story or if I'm just going to work my way through all the water animals one by one.

So one by one all the water animals tried to find the mud at the bottom of the ocean, and all of them failed until the only animal left was Otter. Otter, however, wasn't particularly interested in finding mud.

Is it fun to play with? asked Otter.

Not really, said Charm.

Is it good to eat? asked Otter.

Not really, said Charm.

Then why do you want to find it? said Otter.

For the magic, said Charm.

Oh, said Otter. I like magic.

So Otter took a deep breath and dove into the water. And she didn't come up. Day after day, Charm and the animals waited for Otter to come to the surface. Finally, on the morning of the fourth day, just as the sun was rising, Otter's body floated up out of the depths.

Oh, no, said all the animals, Otter has drowned trying

to find the mud. And they hoisted Otter's body onto the back of the Turtle.

Now, when they hoisted Otter's body onto the back of the Turtle, they noticed that her little paws were clenched shut, and when they opened her paws, they discovered something dark and gooey that wasn't water.

Is this mud? asked the Ducks.

Yes, it is, said Charm. Otter has found the mud.

Of course I found the mud, whispered Otter, who wasn't so much dead as she was tired and out of breath. This magic better be worth it.

Charm set the lump of mud on the back of the Turtle, and she sang and she danced, and the animals sang and danced with her, and very slowly the lump of mud began to grow. It grew and grew and grew into a world, part water, part mud. That was a good trick, said the water animals. But now there's not enough room for all of us in the water. Some of us are going to have to live on land.

Not that anyone wanted to live on the land. It was nothing but mud. Mud as far as the eye could see. Great jumbled lumps of mud.

But before the animals could decide who was going to live where or what to do about the mud-lump world, Charm had her baby.

Or rather, she had her babies.

Twins.

A boy and a girl. One light, one dark. One right-handed, one left-handed.

Nice-looking babies, said the Cormorants. Hope they like mud.

And as it turned out, they did. The right-handed Twin smoothed all the mud lumps until the land was absolutely flat.

Wow! said all the animals. That was pretty clever. Now we can see in all directions.

But before the animals could get used to all the nice flat land, the left-handed Twin stomped around in the mud, piled it up, and created deep valleys and tall mountains.

Okay, said the animals, that could work.

And while the animals were admiring the new land-scape, the Twins really got busy. The right-handed Twin dug nice straight trenches and filled them with water.

.These are rivers, he told the animals, and I've made the water flow in both directions so that it'll be easy to come and go as you please.

That's handy, said the animals.

But as soon as her brother had finished, the left-handed Twin made the rivers crooked and put rocks in the water and made it flow in only one direction.

This is much more exciting, she told the animals.

Could you put in some waterfalls? said the animals. Everyone likes waterfalls.

Sure, said the left-handed Twin. And she did.

The right-handed Twin created forests with all the trees lined up so you could go into the woods and not get lost. The left-handed Twin came along and moved the trees around, so that some of the forest was dense and difficult, and other parts were open and easy.

How about some trees with nuts and fruit? said the animals. In case we get hungry.

That's a good idea, said the right-handed Twin. And he did.

The right-handed Twin created roses. The left-handed Twin put thorns on the stems. The right-handed Twin created summer. The left-handed Twin created winter. The right-handed Twin created sunshine. The left-handed Twin created shadows.

Have we forgotten anything? the Twins asked the animals.

What about human beings? said the animals. Do you think we need human beings?

Why not? said the Twins. And quick as they could the right-handed Twin created women, and the left-handed Twin created men.

They don't look too bright, said the animals. We hope they won't be a problem.

Don't worry, said the Twins, you guys are going to get along just fine.

The animals and the humans and the Twins and Charm looked around at the world that they had created. Boy, they said, this is as good as it gets. This is one beautiful world.

It's a neat story, isn't it? A little long, but different. Maybe even a little exotic. Sort of like the manure-fired pots or the hand-painted plates or the woven palm hats or the coconuts carved to look like monkey faces or the colourful T-shirts that we buy on vacation.

Souvenirs. Snapshots of a moment. And when the moment has passed, the hats are tossed into closets, the

T-shirts are stuffed into drawers, the pots and plates and coconuts are left to gather dust on shelves. Eventually everything is shipped off to a garage sale or slipped into the trash.

As for stories such as the Woman Who Fell from the Sky, well, we listen to them and then we forget them, for amidst the thunder of Christian monologues, they have neither purchase nor place. After all, within the North American paradigm we have a perfectly serviceable creation story.

And it goes like this.

In the beginning God created the heaven and the earth. And the earth was without form, and void and darkness was upon the face of the deep. And the Spirit of God moved upon the face of the waters. And God said, let there be light, and there was light.

You can't beat the King James version of the Bible for the beauty of the language. But it's the story that captures the imagination. God creates night and day, the sun and the moon, all the creatures of the world, and finally, toward the end of his labours, he creates humans. Man first and then woman. Adam and Eve. And he places everything and everyone in a garden, a perfect world. No sickness, no death, no hate, no hunger.

And there's only one rule.

Of every tree of the garden thou mayest freely eat. But of the tree of the knowledge of good and evil, thou shalt not eat of it, for in the day that thou eatest thereof thou shalt surely die.

One rule. Don't break it.

But that's exactly what happens. Adam and Eve break the rule. Doesn't matter how it happens. If you like the orthodox version, you can blame Eve. She eats the apple and brings it back to Adam. Not that Adam says no. A less misogynist reading would blame them both, would chalk up the debacle that followed as an unavoidable mistake. A wrong step. Youthful enthusiasm. A misunderstanding. Wilfulness.

But whatever you wish to call it, the rule has been broken, and that is the end of the garden. God seals it off and places an angel with a fiery sword at the entrance and tosses Adam and Eve into a howling wilderness to fend for themselves, a wilderness in which sickness and death, hate and hunger are their constant companions.

Okay. Two creation stories. One Native, one Christian. The first thing you probably noticed was that I spent more time with the Woman Who Fell from the Sky than I did with Genesis. I'm assuming that most of you have heard of Adam and Eve, but few, I imagine, have ever met Charm. I also used different strategies in the telling of these stories. In the Native story, I tried to recreate an oral storytelling voice and craft the story in terms of a performance for a general audience. In the Christian story, I tried to maintain a sense of rhetorical distance and decorum while organizing the story for a knowledgeable gathering. These strategies colour the stories and suggest values that may be neither inherent nor warranted. In the Native story, the conversational voice tends to highlight the exuberance of the story but diminishes its authority, while the sober voice in the Christian story makes for a formal recitation but creates a sense of veracity.

Basil Johnston, the Anishinabe storyteller, in his essay "How Do We Learn Language?" describes the role of comedy and laughter in stories by reminding us that Native peoples have always loved to laugh: "It is precisely because our tribal stories are comical and evoke laughter that they have never been taken seriously outside the tribe. . . . But behind and beneath the comic characters and the comic situations exists the real meaning of the story . . . what the tribe understood about human growth and development."[3]

Of course, none of you would make the mistake of confusing storytelling strategies with the value or sophistication of a story. And we know enough about the complexities of cultures to avoid the error of imagining animism and polytheism to be no more than primitive versions of monotheism. Don't we?

Nonetheless, the talking animals are a problem.

A theologian might argue that these two creation stories are essentially the same. Each tells about the creation of the world and the appearance of human beings. But a storyteller would tell you that these two stories are quite different, for whether you read the Bible as sacred text or secular metaphor, the elements in Genesis create a particular universe governed by a series of hierarchies — God, man, animals, plants — that celebrate law, order, and good government, while in our Native story, the universe is governed by a series of co-operations — Charm, the

Twins, animals, humans — that celebrate equality and balance.

In Genesis, all creative power is vested in a single deity who is omnipotent, omniscient, and omnipresent. The universe begins with his thought, and it is through his actions and only his actions that it comes into being. In the Earth Diver story, and in many other Native creation stories for that matter, deities are generally figures of limited power and persuasion, and the acts of creation and the decisions that affect the world are shared with other characters in the drama.

In Genesis, we begin with a perfect world, but after the Fall, while we gain knowledge, we lose the harmony and safety of the garden and are forced into a chaotic world of harsh landscapes and dangerous shadows.

In our Native story, we begin with water and mud, and, through the good offices of Charm, her twins, and the animals, move by degrees and adjustments from a formless, featureless world to a world that is rich in its diversity, a world that is complex and complete.

Finally, in Genesis, the post-garden world we inherit is decidedly martial in nature, a world at war — God vs. the Devil, humans vs. the elements. Or to put things into corporate parlance, competitive. In our Native story, the world is at peace, and the pivotal concern is not with the ascendancy of good over evil but with the issue of balance.

So here are our choices: a world in which creation is a solitary, individual act or a world in which creation is a shared activity; a world that begins in harmony and slides toward chaos or a world that begins in chaos and moves toward harmony; a world marked by competition or a world determined by co-operation.

And there's the problem.

If we see the world through Adam's eyes, we are necessarily blind to the world that Charm and the Twins and the animals help to create. If we believe one story to be sacred, we must see the other as secular.

You'll recognize this pairing as a dichotomy, the elemental structure of Western society. And cranky old Jacques Derrida notwithstanding, we do love our dichotomies. Rich/poor, white/black, strong/weak, right/wrong, culture/nature, male/female, written/oral, civilized/barbaric, success/failure, individual/communal. We trust easy oppositions. We are suspicious of complexities, distrustful of contradictions, fearful of enigmas.

Enigmas like my father.

I have a couple of old black-and-white pictures of him holding a baby with my mother looking on. He looks young in those photos. And happy. I'm sure he didn't leave because he hated me, just as I'm sure that my mother didn't stay because she loved me. Yet this is the story I continue to tell myself, because it's easy and contains all my anger, and because, in all the years, in all the tellings, I've honed it sharp enough to cut bone.

If we had to have a patron story for North America, we could do worse than the one about Alexander the Great, who, when faced with the puzzle of the Gordian knot, solved that problem with nothing more than a strong arm and a sharp sword.

Perhaps this is why we delight in telling stories about heroes battling the odds and the elements, rather than about the magic of seasonal change. Why we relish stories that lionize individuals who start at the bottom and fight their way to the top, rather than stories that frame these forms of competition as varying degrees of insanity. Why we tell our children that life is hard, when we could just as easily tell them that it is sweet.

Is it our nature? Do the stories we tell reflect the world as it truly is, or did we simply start off with the wrong story? Like Silko's witches in the cave, conjuring up things to impress each other.

Making magic.

Making faces.

Making mistakes.

I'm dying to remind myself that the basis of Christian doctrine is rectitude and reward, crime and punishment, even though my partner has warned me that this is probably not a good idea. Tell a story, she told me. Don't preach. Don't try to sound profound. It's unbecoming, and you do it poorly. Don't show them your mind. Show them your imagination.

So am I such an ass as to disregard this good advice and suggest that the stories contained within the matrix of Christianity and the complex of nationalism are responsible for the social, political, and economic problems we face? Am I really arguing that the martial and hierarchical nature of Western religion and Western privilege has fostered stories that encourage egotism and self-interest? Am I suggesting that, if we hope to create a truly civil society, we must first burn all the flags and kill all the gods, because in such a world we could no longer tolerate such weapons of mass destruction?

No, I wouldn't do that.

Though certainly we understand that we clear-cut forests not to enrich the lives of animals but to make profit. We know that we dam(n) rivers not to improve water quality but to create electricity and protect private property. We make race and gender discriminatory markers for no other reason than that we can. And we maintain and tolerate poverty not because we believe adversity makes you strong, but because we're unwilling to share.

Ah. You've heard all this before, haven't you.

You may have already leaned over to a friend and whispered, Platitude. Platitude, platitude, platitude. Thomas King the duck-billed platitude.

But give this a thought. What if the creation story in Genesis had featured a flawed deity who was understanding and sympathetic rather than autocratic and rigid? Someone who, in the process of creation, found herself lost from time to time and in need of advice, someone who was willing to accept a little help with the more difficult decisions?

What if the animals had decided on their own names? What if Adam and Eve had simply been admonished for their foolishness?

I love you, God could have said, but I'm not happy with your behaviour. Let's talk this over. Try to do better next time.

What kind of a world might we have created with that kind of story?

Unfortunately, by the time we arrived in the wilderness, broke and homeless, the story of being made in God's image, of living in paradise, of naming the animals must have gone to our heads, for while we weren't the strongest or the fastest or the fiercest creatures on the planet, we were, certainly, as it turned out, the most arrogant.

God's Chosen People. The Alpha and the Omega. Masters of the Universe.

It is this conceit we continue to elaborate as we fill up our tanks at the gas station, the myth we embrace as we bolt our doors at night, the romance we pursue as we search our guidebooks for just the right phrase. The lie we dangle in front of our appetites as we chase progress to the grave.

Or as Linda McQuaig so delightfully puts it in her book *All You Can Eat: Greed, Lust and the New Capitalism*, "The central character in economics is Homo Economicus, the human prototype, who is pretty much just a walking set of insatiable material desires. He uses his rational abilities to ensure the satisfaction of all his wants, which are the key to his motivation. And he isn't considered some weirdo; the whole point of him is that he represents traits basic to all of us — Homo Economicus 'R' Us, as it were."[4]

It was Sir Isaac Newton who said, "To every action there is always opposed an equal reaction." Had he been a writer, he might have simply said, "To every action there is a story."

Take Charm's story, for instance. It's yours. Do with it what you will. Tell it to friends. Turn it into a television movie. Forget it. But don't say in the years to come that you would have lived your life differently if only you had heard this story.

You've heard it now.

II

YOU'RE NOT THE INDIAN
I HAD IN MIND

THERE IS A STORY I KNOW. It's about the earth and how it floats in space on the back of a turtle. I've heard this story many times, and each time someone tells the story, it changes. Sometimes the change is simply in the voice of the storyteller. Sometimes the change is in the details. Sometimes in the order of events. Other times it's the dialogue or the response of the audience. But in all the tellings of all the tellers, the world never leaves the turtle's back. And the turtle never swims away.

One time, it was in Lethbridge I think, a young boy in the audience asked about the turtle and the earth. If the earth was on the back of the turtle, what was below the turtle? Another turtle, the storyteller told him. And below that turtle? Another turtle. And below that? Another turtle.

The boy began to laugh, enjoying the game, I imagine. So how many turtles are there? he wanted to know. The storyteller shrugged. No one knows for sure, she told him, but it's turtles all the way down.

The truth about stories is that that's all we are. "You can't understand the world without telling a story," the Anishinabe writer Gerald Vizenor tells us. "There isn't any center to the world but a story."[1]

In 1994, I came up with the bright idea of travelling around North America and taking black-and-white portraits of Native artists. For a book. A millennium project. I figured I'd spend a couple of months each year on the road travelling to cities and towns and reserves in Canada and the United States, and when 2000 rolled around, there I'd be with a terrific coffee-table book to welcome the next thousand years.

I should tell you that I had not come up with this idea on my own. As a matter of fact, Edward Sheriff Curtis had already done it. Photographed Indians, that is. Indeed, Curtis is probably the most famous of the Indian photographers. He started his project of photographing the Indians of North America around 1900, and for the next thirty years he roamed the continent, producing some forty thousand negatives, of which more than twenty-two hundred were published.

Curtis was fascinated by the idea of the North American Indian, obsessed with it. And he was determined to capture that idea, that image, before it vanished. This was a common concern among many intellectuals and artists and social scientists at the turn of the nineteenth century, who believed that, while Europeans in the New World were poised on the brink of a new adventure, the Indian was poised on the brink of extinction.

In literature in the United States, this particular span of time is known as the American Romantic Period, and the Indian was tailor-made for it. With its emphasis on feeling, its interest in nature, its fascination with exoticism, mysticism, and eroticism, and its preoccupation with the glorification of the past, American Romanticism found in the Indian a symbol in which all these concerns could be united. Prior to the nineteenth century, the prevalent image of the Indian had been that of an inferior being. The Romantics imagined their Indian as dying. But in that dying, in that passing away, in that disappearing from the stage of human progress, there was also a sense of nobility.

One of the favourite narrative strategies was to create a single, heroic Indian (male, of course) — James Fenimore Cooper's Chingachgook, John Augustus Stone's Metamora, Henry Wadsworth Longfellow's Hiawatha — who was the last of his race. Indeed, during this period, death and nobility were sympathetic ideas that complemented one another, and writers during the first half of the nineteenth century used them in close association, creating a literary shroud in which to wrap the Indian. And bury him.

Edgar Allan Poe believed that the most poetic topic in the world was the death of a beautiful woman. From the literature produced during the nineteenth century, second place would have to go to the death of the Indian.

Not that Indians were dying. To be sure, while many

of the tribes who lived along the east coast of North America, in the interior of Lower Canada, and in the Connecticut, Ohio, and St. Lawrence river valleys had been injured and disoriented by the years of almost continuous warfare, by European diseases, and by the destructive push of settlers for cheap land, the vast majority of the tribes were a comfortable distance away from the grave.

This was the Indian of fact.

In 1830, when the American president, Andrew Jackson, fulfilling an election promise to his western and southern supporters, pushed the Removal Act through Congress, he did so in order to get rid of thousands of Indians — particularly the Cherokees, Choctaws, Chickasaws, Creeks, and Seminoles — who were not dying and not particularly interested in going anywhere.

These were not the Indians Curtis went west to find.

Curtis was looking for the literary Indian, the dying Indian, the imaginative construct. And to make sure that he would find what he wanted to find, he took along boxes of "Indian" paraphernalia — wigs, blankets, painted backdrops, clothing — in case he ran into Indians who did not look as the Indian was supposed to look.

I collect postcards. Old ones, new ones. Postcards that depict Indians or Indian subjects. I have one from the 1920s that shows an Indian lacrosse team in Oklahoma. Another is a hand-coloured rendering of the Sherman Indian School in California. A third is a cartoon of an Indian man fishing in the background while, in the foreground, a tourist takes a picture of the man's wife and their seven kids with the rather puerile caption "And what does the chief do when he's not fishing?"

One of my favourites is a photograph of a group of Indians, in full headdresses, golfing at the Banff Springs Hotel golf course in 1903. The photograph was taken by Byron Harmon and shows Jim Brewster and Norman Luxton, two Banff locals, caddying for what looks to be five Indians who are identified only as "two Stoney Indian Chiefs." I like this particular postcard because there is an element of play in the image of Indians in beaded outfits and full headdresses leaning on their golf clubs while their horses graze in the background, and because I can't tell if the person on the tee with bobbed hair, wearing what looks to be a dress and swinging the club, is an Indian or a White, a man or a woman.

But the vast majority of my postcards offer no such mysteries. They are simply pictures and paintings of Indians in feathers and leathers, sitting in or around tipis or chasing buffalo on pinto ponies.

Some of these postcards are old, but many of them are brand new, right off the rack. Two are contemporary pieces from the Postcard Factory in Markham, Ontario. The first shows an older Indian man in a full beaded and fringed leather outfit with an eagle feather war bonnet and a lance, sitting on a horse, set against a backdrop of trees and mountains. The second is a group of five Indians, one older man in a full headdress sitting on a horse and four younger men on foot: two with bone breastplates, one with a leather vest, and one bare chested.

The interesting thing about these two postcards is that the solitary man on his horse is identified only as a "Cree Indian," while the group of five is designated as "Native Indians," much like the golfers, as if none of them had names or identities other than the cliché. Though to give them identities, to reveal them to be actual people, would be, I suppose, a violation of the physical laws governing matter and antimatter, that the Indian and Indians cannot exist in the same imagination.

Which must be why the White caddies on the Banff postcard have names.

And the Indians do not.

It is my postcard Indian that Curtis was after. And in spite of the fact that Curtis met a great variety of Native people who would have given the lie to the construction, in spite of the fact that he fought vigorously for Native rights and published articles and books that railed against the government's treatment of Indians, this was the Indian that Curtis believed in.

I probably sound a little cranky. I don't mean to. I know Curtis paid Indians to shave away any facial hair. I know he talked them into wearing wigs. I know that he would provide one tribe of Indians with clothing from another tribe because the clothing looked more "Indian."

So his photographs would look authentic.

And while there is a part of me that would have preferred that Curtis had photographed his Indians as he found them, the men with crewcuts and moustaches, the women in cotton print dresses, I am grateful that we have his images at all, for the faces of the mothers and fathers, aunts and uncles, sisters and brothers who look at you from the depths of these photographs are not romantic illusions, they are real people.

Native culture, as with any culture, is a vibrant, changing thing, and when Curtis happened upon it, it was changing from what it had been to what it would become next. But the idea of "the Indian" was already fixed in time and space. Even before Curtis built his first camera, that image had been set. His task as he visited tribe after tribe was to sort through what he saw in order to find what he needed.

But to accuse Curtis of romantic myopia is to be petty and to ignore the immensity of the project and the personal and economic ordeal that he undertook. He spent his life photographing and writing about Indians. He died harnessed to that endeavour, and, when I look at his photographs, I can imagine this solitary man moving across the prairies, through the forests, along the coast, dragging behind him an enormous camera and tripod and the cultural expectations of an emerging nation, and I am humbled.

So when I set out in the fall of 1995 on what I had pompously decided to call the Medicine River Photographic Expedition, I was stuffed full of high expectations. My brother Christopher, who is a fine woodworker and three years younger than I, wanted to come along. He told me that the expedition sounded like fun and the prospect of meeting other Native artists was appealing.

My mother, fearful that her only children might get lost in the heart of the heart of the country, cooked and packed us six roast chickens, twenty dozen chocolate chip cookies, an entire tree of bananas, a vineyard of grapes, an orchard of apples and oranges, four loaves of bread, a case of drinking water, candy (in case we ran out of cookies, I guess), and four pounds of butter. Along with a complete set of maps of the provinces and states, three flashlights of varying sizes, a highway hazard warning light, a car-battery charging system with an electrical tire inflater, several pamphlets on how to survive in the wilderness, and a compass.

After we had packed and said our goodbyes, she walked alongside the car all the way to the street and had us roll down the window so she could tell us to drive carefully.

As we slipped onto the interstate, the Volvo stuffed with camera gear and the better part of a grocery store, and began following my bright idea down to the American Southwest, I can remember thinking that Curtis couldn't have been any better outfitted.

In Roseville, California, where I grew up, race was little more than a series of cultural tributaries that flowed through the town, coming together in confluences, swinging away into eddies. There were at least three main streams, Mexicans, the Mediterranean folk — Italians and Greeks — and the general mix of Anglo-Saxons that a Japanese friend of mine, years later, would refer to as the Crazy Caucasoids. But in Roseville in the late 1950s and early 1960s, there were no Asian families that I can remember, and the picture I have of my 1961 graduating class does not contain a single black face.

If there was a racial divide in the town, it was the line between the Mexicans and everyone else. Some of the Mexican families had been in the area long before California fell to the Americans in 1848 as a spoil of war. The rest had come north later to work the fields and had settled in Roseville and the other small towns — Elk Grove, Lodi, Stockton, Turlock, Merced, Fresno — that ran through the heart of the Sacramento and San Joaquin valleys.

I went to school with Hernandezes and Gomezes. But I didn't socialize with them, didn't even know where they lived. My brother and I kept pretty much to our own neighbourhood, a five- or six-block area on the north-western edge of town bounded by auction yards and an ocean of open fields.

Racism is a funny thing, you know. Dead quiet on occasion. Often dangerous. But sometimes it has a peculiar sense of humour. The guys I ran with looked at Mexicans with a certain disdain. I'd like to say that I didn't, but that wasn't true. No humour here. Except that while I was looking at Mexicans, other people, as it turned out, were looking at me.

In my last year of high school, I mustered enough courage to ask Karen Butler to go to the prom with me. That's not her real name, of course. I've changed it so I don't run the risk of embarrassing her for something that wasn't her fault.

I should probably begin by saying that at eighteen, I was not the prettiest of creatures. Tall and skinny, with no more co-ordination than a three-legged stepladder, I also had drawn the pimple card to brighten my adolescence.

Pimples. The word has an almost dainty sound to it. Like "dimples." But my pimples were not annoying little flares that appeared here and there but rather large, erupting pustules that hurled magma and spewed lava. They crowded against the sides of my nose, burrowed around my lips, and spread out across my chin and forehead like a cluster of volcanic islands.

Roseville was a railroad town. Until the hospital and the shopping centre were built on the southeast side, most everyone lived north of the tracks. Karen was from the south side, one of the new subdivisions, what cultural theorists in the late twentieth century would call "havens of homogeneity."

Karen's mother was a schoolteacher. Her father was a doctor. My mother ran a small beauty shop out of a converted garage. Karen's family was upper middle class. We weren't. Still, there was a levelling of sorts, for Karen had a heart defect. It didn't affect her so far as I could tell, but I figured that being well off with a heart defect was pretty much the same as being poor with pimples. So I asked her if she wanted to go to the prom with me, and she said yes.

Then about a week before the big evening, Karen called me to say that she couldn't go to the dance after all. I'm sorry, she told me. It's my father. He doesn't want me dating Mexicans.

It took my brother and me four days to drive to New Mexico. We could have made the trip in three days, but we kept getting sidetracked by interesting stops. My favourite was a McDonald's on the Will Rogers Turnpike near Claremore, Oklahoma. I generally avoid places like McDonald's but this one had a tiny Will Rogers museum on the first floor of the restaurant, as well a statue of Rogers himself in the parking lot standing next to a flag-pole, twirling a rope.

Tourists pulling off the turnpike and seeing the statue for the first time would probably think Rogers was some kind of famous cowboy. In fact, he was a famous Indian, a sort of Indian/cowboy, a Cherokee to be exact.

But most importantly, he was what the political and literary theorist Antonio Gramsci called an "organic" intellectual, an individual who articulates the under-standings of a community or a nation. During the 1930s Rogers was probably the most famous man in North America. He performed in circuses and Wild West shows. He starred in the Ziegfeld Follies, and from 1933 to 1935 he was the top male motion-picture box-office attraction. Over forty million people read his newspaper columns on everything from gun control to Congress, and even more listened to his weekly radio show. He did just about everything with the exception of running for office. "I ain't going to try that," he said. "I've got some pride left."

Rogers was born near Claremore, Oklahoma, and his family was prominent in the Cherokee Nation. But he didn't look Indian. Not in that constructed way. Certainly not in the way Curtis wanted Indians to look.

And tourists pulling into the parking lot and seeing the statue for the first time would never know that this was an Indian as famous as Sitting Bull or Crazy Horse or Geronimo.

Christopher must have read my mind. The Indians we're going to photograph, he said, walking over to the statue. What if they all look like Rogers? I know he's Indian, said my brother, and you know he's Indian, but how is anyone else going to be able to tell?

Curtis wasn't the only photographer in the early twentieth century who was taking pictures of Indians. So was Richard Throssel. Unless you're a photography buff, you won't know the name and will therefore have no way of knowing that Throssel was not only a contemporary of Curtis's, but that he was also Native. Cree to be exact. Adopted by the Crow. Throssel even met Curtis, when Curtis came to the Crow reservation.

Throssel took many of the same sort of romantic photographs as Curtis, photographs such as "The Sentinel," which shows an Indian in a feathered headdress, holding a lance, and sitting on a horse, all in silhouette, set against a dramatic sky, or "The Feathered Horsemen," which records a party of Indians on horses coming through a stand of tipis, the men wearing feathered headdresses and carrying bows and arrows and lances.

But he also took other photographs, photographs that moved away from romance toward environmental and social comment, photographs that did not imagine the Indian as dying or particularly noble, photographs that suggested that Indians were contemporary as well as historical figures. His photograph of Bull Over the Hill's home titled "The Old and the New," which shows a log house with a tipi in the background, and his 1910 photograph "Interior of the Best Indian Kitchen on the Crow Reservation," which shows an Indian family dressed in "traditional" clothing sitting at an elegantly set table in their very contemporary house having tea, suggest that Native people could negotiate the past and the present with relative ease. His untitled camp scene that juxtaposes traditional tipis with contemporary buggies and a family of pigs, rather than with unshod ponies and the prerequisite herd of buffalo, suggests, at least to my contemporary sensibilities, that Throssel had a penchant for satiric play.

But I'm probably imagining the humour. Throssel was, after all, a serious photographer trying to capture a moment, perhaps not realizing that tripping the shutter captures nothing, that everything on the ground glass changes before the light hits the film plane. What the camera allows you to do is to invent, to create. That's really what photographs are. Not records of moments, but rather imaginative acts.

Still, neither Curtis nor Throssel had to deal with the Rogers conundrum. Or perhaps neither chose to. Throssel's Indians, even the ones set against contemporary backdrops, were, like Curtis's Indians, all visually Indian. And when we look at his photographs, we see what we expect to see.

The Choctaw-Cherokee-Irish writer Louis Owens, in

his memoir *I Hear the Train: Reflections, Inventions, Refractions*, deals with the issue of photographs and expectations. Looking through a collection of old photographs of his mixed-blood family, Owens can find no "Indians." "This family from whom I am descended," he says, "wears no recognizably Indian cultural artifacts; nor are they surrounded by any such signifiers. (Though there is possibility in the blanket nailed across the cabin door: what if my great-grandfather had perversely wrapped the blanket around himself for this picture?) . . . To find the Indian in the photographic cupboard, I must narratively construct him out of his missing presence, for my great-grandfather was Indian but not *an Indian*."[2]

Of course, all this — my expedition, Throssel's images, Owens's family portraits — are reminders of how hard it is to break free from the parochial and paradoxical considerations of identity and authenticity. Owens, in a particularly wry moment, notes that "few looking at [these] photos of mixedbloods would be likely to say, 'But they don't look like Irishmen,' but everyone seems obligated to offer an opinion regarding the degree of Indianness represented."[3]

In Curtis's magnum opus, *Portraits from North American Indian Life*, we don't see a collection of photographs of Indian people. We see race. Never mind that race is a construction and an illusion. Never mind that it does not exist in either biology or theology, though both have, from time to time, been enlisted in the cause of racism. Never mind that we can't hear it or smell it or taste it or feel it. The important thing is that we believe we can see it.

In fact, we hope we can see it. For one of the conundrums of the late twentieth century that we've hauled into the twenty-first is that many of our mothers and fathers, who were pursued by missionaries, educators, and government officials (armed with residential schools, European history, legislation such as the Indian Act, the Termination Act, and the Relocation Program of the 1950s), who were forcibly encouraged to give up their identities, now have children who are *determined* to be *seen* as Indians. Louis Owens isn't the only Native person who has sorted through old photographs and looked in cold mirrors for that visual confirmation.

When I was going to university, there was an almost irresistible pull to become what Gerald Vizenor calls a "cultural ritualist," a kind of "pretend" Indian, an Indian who has to dress up like an Indian and act like an Indian in order to be recognized as an Indian. And in the 1970s, being recognized as an Indian was critical. And here tribal affiliation was not a major consideration. We didn't dress up as nineteenth-century Cherokees or as the Apache, Choctaw, Lakota, Tlingit, Ojibway, Blackfoot, or Haida had dressed. We dressed up as the "Indian" dressed. We dressed up in a manner to substantiate the cultural lie that had trapped us, and we did so with a passion. I have my own box of photographs. Pictures of me in my "Indian" outfits, pictures of me being "Indian," pictures of me in groups of other "Indians."

Not wanting to be mistaken for a Mexican or a White, I grew my hair long, bought a fringed leather pouch to hang off my belt, threw a four-strand bone choker around my neck, made a headband out of an old neckerchief, and strapped on a beaded belt buckle that I had bought at a trading post on a reservation in Wyoming. Trinkets of the trade.

I did resist feathers but that was my only concession to cultural sanity.

Not that university was my first experience with the narrow parameters of race. In 1964, I fell into a job as a junior executive at the Bank of America in San Francisco. Junior executive sounds grand, but as I discovered after the first few days, this was what the bank called men who worked as tellers, as opposed to the women who worked as tellers and who were just called tellers. These terms, though I didn't understand it at the time, were innate promises that men had possibilities of advancement, while women did not.

In any case, it was a boring job, and by the end of the first month I was looking for another career. I didn't find it, but I did meet a woman who worked for a steamship company. Each week, on Friday, she would come in and deposit the company's earnings. I was bored. She was bored. So we talked. The steamship company she worked for was called Columbus Lines, an irony that was not lost on me, and, occasionally, she told me, they would take on "passengers" who could earn their one-way passage to Australia by working aboard the ship.

As it happened, I knew quite a bit about Australia. Just before I moved to San Francisco, I had worked at South Shore Lake Tahoe, a gambling, fun-in-the-sun mecca in the

Sierra Nevada Mountains, where I had dated a woman from Australia. Her name was Sharon or Sherry and she told me all about the country, its beaches, the outback, the sharks. To hear her tell it, the place was bristling with adventure, and, three weeks into our relationship, I applied for an immigration visa. At eight weeks our relationship was over. At the twelve-week mark, just as I was packing to go to San Francisco, my visa arrived. I put it in the box with the books and forgot about it.

Amazing the way things come around.

The next week I asked the woman from the steamship company what the chances were of my getting a one-way job on one of the company's ships, and she told me she thought they were good. I must admit I could hardly contain my excitement.

Tom King, on a tramp steamer. Tom King, sailing off on a great adventure. Tom King, explorer of known worlds.

So I was disappointed when she came back the next week to tell me that the list of people who wanted to work their way to Australia was quite long and that nothing would come open for at least a year. However, there was a ship sailing for New Zealand in a week, and there was one spot left on the crew. If I wanted it, she said, it was mine.

And so I went. Packed everything I owned into two cheap metal trunks and hauled them to the docks. By the end of the week, I was at sea.

The ship was a German vessel out of Hamburg, the SS *Cap Colorado*. The captain was German. The crew was German. The cook was German. I wasn't German. As a matter of fact, none of the crew was sure what I was. When I told them I was Cherokee, or to keep matters simple, a North American Indian, they were intrigued.

And suspicious.

The cook, who could speak passable English, told me that he had read all of Karl May's novels and had a fair idea of what Indians were supposed to look like and that I wasn't what he had imagined.

"You're not the Indian I had in mind," he told me.

Here was a small dilemma. Of all the crew members on that ship, the one person I didn't want to offend was the cook. I knew that Indians came in all shapes and sizes and colours, but I hadn't read Karl May, had no idea who he was. The cook had read May but had never actually seen an Indian. So we compromised. I confessed that I was a mixed-blood, and he allowed that this was possible, since May had described full-blood Apaches and not mixed-blood Cherokees.

I discovered some years later that May had never seen an Indian, either, but on board that ship it was probably just as well that I did not know this.

I spent almost a year in New Zealand. I worked as a deer culler, a beer bottle sorter, a freezer packer, and a photographer. I liked the country and might well have stayed had it not been for a phone call I got early one morning. It was a British-sounding man who introduced himself as an official with the immigration department.

If I'm not mistaken, he said, clipping the edges off each consonant, you entered the country eleven months ago on a thirty-day tourist visa and are therefore in violation of New Zealand immigration laws.

I agreed that he was probably correct.

When might we expect you to leave? he wanted to know.

As I said, I liked the place, had no plans to leave. So I asked him if there was any chance of applying for an immigration visa.

It turned out my immigration man had only newly arrived from England the month before to take up his duties and wasn't sure if this was possible. But he would check into it, he told me. In the meantime, would I give him some of my particulars.

It was the usual stuff. Name. Colour of hair. Colour of eyes. Height. Weight. Race.

Black, brown, six feet six inches, 230 pounds.

Indian.

Dear me, he said. I don't believe we take applications from Indians.

I have to admit I was stunned. Why not? I wanted to know.

Policy, said the immigration man.

Do you get many? I asked.

Oh, yes, he said. Thousands.

I hadn't heard of any mass exodus of Native peoples from Canada or the States. These Indians, I asked him, where are they from? Alberta? Saskatchewan? Arizona? South Dakota? Oklahoma?

Dear me, no, said my British voice. They're from, you know, New Delhi, Bombay . . .

When Karen told me her father wouldn't let me take her to the prom because he didn't want her dating Mexicans, I told her I wasn't Mexican. I was Indian.

When the immigration officer told me I couldn't apply for a visa because I was Indian, I told him I wasn't East Indian, I was North American Indian.

As if that was going to settle anything.

Without missing a beat, and at the same time injecting a note of enthusiasm into his otherwise precise voice, the immigration man said, What? Do you mean like cowboys and Indians?

The next week, I was on a ship for Australia. As it turned out, that immigration visa I had was still good. As for Karen, well, I went to the prom that year. But I went alone.

The first three or four months I was in Australia, I travelled around, working my way up the east coast and into the interior. At Rockhampton, I made pocket money helping a man and his son dismantle a small house. At Tennent Creek, I worked at a mine shovelling ore into sacks. In Adelaide, I cleaned trucks. But in all my travels, I never met an indigenous Australian. In New Zealand, I had met a great many Maoris, and while there had been friction between Maoris and Europeans, the two groups seemed to have organized themselves around an uneasy peace between equals. In Australia, there was no such peace. Just a damp, sweltering campaign of discrimination that you could feel on your skin and smell in your hair.

The Aboriginal people, I was told, were failing. They were dying off at such a rate that they wouldn't last another decade. It was sad to see them passing away, but their problem, according to the men who gathered in the bars after work, was that they did not have the same mental capacities as Whites. There was no point in educating them because they had no interest in improving their lot and were perfectly happy living in poverty and squalor.

The curious thing about these stories was I had heard them all before, knew them, in fact, by heart.

Eventually I wound up in Sydney and lied my way into a job as a journalist with a third-rate magazine called *Everybody's* — a disingenuous name if ever there was one. I got the job, in part, because I was an American and an Indian — the exotic combination being too much for folks to resist — and I was sent out on jobs that required the firm hand of a reporter of exotic background. I filed stories about teenagers having a good time drinking themselves into a stupor and jumping off cliffs into the ocean, about escorting a chimpanzee around the city and showing her the sights, about spending an exhilarating afternoon with the self-proclaimed king of tic-tac-toe, discussing strategies and secret moves.

Almost certainly, the high point of my journalistic career was dragging one of those plastic blow-up dollies around on a date that included dinner and a movie. You'll probably think poorly of me, but I didn't really mind doing these idiotic assignments. Actually, many of them were fun. Best of all, I had a professional job. Race, which had periodically been something of a burden, was suddenly something of an advantage.

There was a photographer who worked for the magazine. Let's say that, after all these years, I've forgotten his name. So, we'll call him Lee. Lee was a decent enough guy, but on Friday afternoons when we got paid and adjourned to the local pub to drink and review the week, he would turn into a boor. The kind of boor who, after half a dozen beers and a few whisky chasers, liked to expound on what was wrong with the country. Government was at the top of his list, followed closely by Australia's "Abo" problem — "Abo" being Australia's derogatory term for the Aboriginal people. And because there were no Aboriginal people in the immediate vicinity, Lee spent many of these smoky evenings sharpening his soggy wit on me.

Lee didn't know any more about Indians than had the cook on the tramp steamer or Karl May or the immigration man, but he reckoned that North Americans had taken care of the problem in a reasonably expedient fashion. I'm embarrassed to repeat his exact words but the gist of it was that North Americans had shot Native men and bred Native women until they were White.

In a perverse way, I've always liked people like Lee. They are, by and large, easy to deal with. Their racism is honest and straightforward. You don't have to go looking for it in a phrase or a gesture. And you don't have to wonder if you're being too sensitive. Best of all, they remind me how the past continues to inform the present.

One Monday, Lee stopped by my desk with a present

for me. It was a cartoon that he had gotten one of the guys in the art department to work up. It showed a stereotypical Indian in feathers and leathers with a bull's eye on his crotch and flies buzzing around him. "Office of Chief Screaching [*sic*] Eagle Goldstein," the caption read. "Payola and bribes acceptable in the form of checks or money orders. No silver please." Just above the Indian was "Happy Barmizvah Keemosaby" and just below was "only living Cherokee Jew."

Lee stood at my desk, waiting for me to smile. I told him it was funny as hell, and he said, yeah, everyone he had showed it to thought it was a scream. I had the cartoon mounted on a board and stuck it on my desk.

I still have it. Just in case I forget.

So it was unanimous. Everyone knew who Indians were. Everyone knew what we looked like. Even Indians. But standing in that parking lot in Oklahoma with my brother, looking at the statue of Will Rogers, I realized, for perhaps the first time, that I didn't know. Or more accurately, I didn't know how I wanted to represent Indians. My brother was right. Will Rogers did not look like an Indian. Worse, as I cast my mind across the list of Native artists I had come west to photograph, many of them friends, I realized that a good number of them didn't look Indian, either.

Yet how can something that has never existed — the Indian — have form and power while something that is alive and kicking — Indians — are invisible?

Edward Sheriff Curtis.

James Fenimore Cooper, George Catlin, Paul Kane, Charles Bird King, Karl May, the Atlanta Braves, the Washington Redskins, the Chicago Blackhawks, Pontiac (the car, not the Indian), Land O'Lakes butter, Calumet baking soda, Crazy Horse Malt Liquor, *A Man Called Horse*, Iron Eyes Cody, *Dances with Wolves*, *The Searchers*, the Indian Motorcycle Company, American Spirit tobacco, Native American Barbie, Chippewa Springs Golf Course, John Augustus Stone, the Cleveland Indians, Disney's Pocahontas, Geronimo shoes, the Calgary Stampede, Cherokee brand underwear, the Improved Order of Red Men, Ralph Hubbard and his Boy Scout troop, Mutual of Omaha, Buffalo Bill's Wild West Show, the Boston Tea Party, Frank Hamilton Cushing, William Wadsworth Longfellow, the Bank of Montreal, Chief's Trucking, Grey Owl, *The Sioux Spaceman*, Red Man chewing tobacco, Grateful Dead concerts, Dreamcatcher perfume.

In the end, there is no reason for the Indian to be real. The Indian simply has to exist in our imaginations.

But for those of us who are Indians, this disjunction between reality and imagination is akin to life and death. For to be seen as "real," for people to "imagine" us as Indians, we must be "authentic."

In the past, authenticity was simply in the eye of the beholder. Indians who looked Indian were authentic. Authenticity only became a problem for Native people in the twentieth century. While it is true that mixed-blood and full-blood rivalries predate this period, the question of who was an Indian and who was not was easier to settle. What made it easy was that most Indians lived on reserves of one sort or another (out of sight of Europeans) and had strong ties to a particular community, and the majority of those people who "looked Indian" and those who did not at least had a culture and a language in common.

This is no longer as true as it once was, for many Native people now live in cities, with only tenuous ties to a reserve or a nation. Many no longer speak their Native language, a gift of colonialism, and the question of identity has become as much a personal matter as it is a matter of blood. N. Scott Momaday has suggested that being Native is an idea that an individual has of themselves. Momaday, who is Kiowa, is not suggesting that anyone who wants to can imagine themselves to be Indian. He is simply acknowledging that language and narrow definitions of culture are not the only ways identity can be constructed. Yet, in the absence of visual confirmation, these "touchstones" — race, culture, language, blood — still form a kind of authenticity test, a racial-reality game that contemporary Native people are forced to play. And here are some of the questions.

Were you born on a reserve? Small, rural towns with high Native populations will do. Cities will not.

Do you speak your Native language? Not a few phrases here and there. Fluency is the key. No fluency, no Indian.

Do you participate in your tribe's ceremonies? Being a singer or a dancer is a plus, but not absolutely required.

Are you a full-blood?

Are you a status Indian?

Are you enrolled?

You may suspect me of hyperbole, but many of these were questions that I was asked by a selection committee when I applied for a Ford Foundation Grant for American Indians in order to complete my Ph.D. I've told this story a number of times at various events, and each time I've told it, one or two non-Natives have come up to me afterwards and apologized for the stereotypical attitudes of a few misguided Whites. But the truth of the matter is that the selection committee was composed entirely of Native people. And the joke, if there is one, is that most of the committee couldn't pass this test, either, for these questions were not designed to measure academic potential or to ensure diversity, they were designed to exclude. For the real value of authenticity is in the rarity of a thing.

Of course, outside grant selection committees and possibly guards at the new and improved U.S. border crossings, not many people ask these questions. They don't have to. They're content simply looking at you. If you don't look Indian, you aren't. If you don't look White, you're not.

As I pulled out of the McDonald's parking lot, I began thinking about my dilemma in earnest. Edward Sheriff Curtis had been successful in raising money and getting his photographs in print because he was fulfilling a national fantasy, and because he documented the only antiquity that North America would ever have. Indians might not have been Greeks or Romans or Egyptians, but Indians were all the continent had to offer to a society that relished the past. I could not photograph that particular antiquity, not because it had vanished, but because it had changed.

When I came up with my bright idea for a photographic expedition, I sat down with a number of granting agencies to see if there was any chance of getting some financial support for the project. Several of them thought the idea had merit, but they weren't sure why I wanted to do it.

Which Indians did I have in mind, they wanted to know. How would I find these Indians? How would taking photographs of Native artists benefit Native people?

Had J. P. Morgan asked that question of Edward Curtis, Curtis probably would have told him that such photographs were necessary because the Indian was dying, and if he hesitated, the Noble Red Man would be gone and that part of America's antiquity would be lost forever. Curtis might have even thrown up John Audubon and Audubon's great endeavour to paint the birds of North America, many of whom were on the verge of extinction and might well have been helped on their way, since, in order to paint the birds, Audubon first had to kill them.

So they wouldn't move and spoil the sitting.

How will taking photographs of Native artists benefit Native people?

It wasn't a question I would have ever asked. It was a question — and I understood this part clearly — that came out of a Western Judeo-Christian sense of responsibility and that contained the unexamined implication that the lives of Native people needed improvement. I knew, without a doubt, that the pictures I was taking would not change the lives of the people I photographed any more than the arrivals and departures of, say, anthropologists on Native reserves had done anything to improve the lives of the people they came to study.

I teach at a university, so I know all about the enthusiasm for creating social change through intellectual and artistic activity, especially within what we ironically call the "humanities." And while we have had our fair share of literary critics who have believed in the potentials of literature — Sir Philip Sidney, Matthew Arnold, F. R. and Queenie Leavis — it goes without saying, I think, that, apart from recent feminist and Marxist critics who seek to engage literature in the enterprise of social and political transformation, the study of literature, especially in the wake of New Criticism, has not had a sustained political component.

So I was, in many ways, delighted to see postcolonial studies arrive on campus, not only because it expanded the canon by insisting that we read, consider, and teach the literatures of colonized peoples, but because it promised to give Native people a place at the table. I know that postcolonial studies is not a panacea for much of anything. I know that it never promised explicitly to make the colonized world a better place for colonized peoples. It did, however, carry with it the implicit expectation that, through exposure to new literatures and cultures and challenges to hegemonic assumptions and power structures, lives would be made better.

At least the lives of the theorists.

But perhaps that was it. Perhaps I was travelling around the country taking portraits of Native artists because the project promised to make my life better, to make me feel valuable, to make me feel important.

How will photographing Native artists benefit Native people? You see this basic kind of question in various guises on the "human study" portion of grant applications, and you hear it debated on talk shows and in churches. Politicians use it as a ploy because they know that political memory is not even short term. Advertisers transform the question into a glimmering promise that if you buy their products — deodorants, frozen pizzas, magic beans — your life will improve. It is the great Western come-on. The North American Con. The Caucasoid Sting.

Actually, I'm no better. If you've been paying attention, you will have noticed that I've defined identity politics in a rather narrow and self-serving fashion.

Appearance.

I want to look Indian so that you will see me as Indian because I want to be Indian, even though being Indian and looking Indian is more a disadvantage than it is a luxury.

Just not for me.

Middle-class Indians, such as myself, can, after all, afford the burden of looking Indian. There's little danger that *we'll* be stuffed into the trunk of a police cruiser and dropped off on the outskirts of Saskatoon. Not much chance that *we'll* come before the courts and be incarcerated for a longer period of time than our non-Indian brethren. Hardly any risk that *our* children will be taken from us because we are unable to cope with the potentials of poverty.

That sort of thing happens to those other Indians.

My relatives. My friends.

Just not me.

To date, I've photographed about five hundred Native artists. In that time some of the people, such as the Navajo artist Carl Gorman, have died. Before I finish, more will pass away, and new ones will take their place. I may never finish the project, may never see the book I had imagined when my brother and I headed off that first time almost ten years ago. But it doesn't matter. The photographs themselves are no longer the issue. Neither are the questions of identity. What's important are the stories I've heard along the way. And the stories I've told. Stories we make up to try to set the world straight.

Take Will Rogers's story, for instance. It's yours. Do with it what you will. Make it the topic of a discussion group at a scholarly conference. Put it on the Web. Forget it. But don't say in the years to come that you would have lived your life differently if only you had heard this story.

You've heard it now.

III

LET ME ENTERTAIN YOU

THERE IS A STORY I KNOW. It's about the earth and how it floats in space on the back of a turtle. I've heard this story many times, and each time someone tells the story, it changes. Sometimes the change is simply in the voice of the storyteller. Sometimes the change is in the details. Sometimes in the order of events. Other times it's the dialogue or the response of the audience. But in all the tellings of all the tellers, the world never leaves the turtle's back. And the turtle never swims away.

One time, it was in Peterborough I think, an older woman in the audience asked about the turtle and the earth. If the earth was on the back of a turtle, what was below the turtle? Another turtle, the storyteller told her. And below that turtle? Another turtle. And below that? Another turtle.

The woman began to smile, enjoying the game, I imagine. So how many turtles are there? she wanted to know. The storyteller shrugged. No one knows for sure, he told her, but it's turtles all the way down.

The truth about stories is that that's all we are. The Metis singer Andrea Menard reminds us of this in the first verse of her song "The Halfbreed Blues."

> I was born the privileged skin.
> And my eyes are bright, bright brown
> You'd never know there is Metis blood
> Raging underground
> Let me tell you a story about a revelation.
> It's not the colour of a nation that holds a nation's pride
> It's imagination.
> It's imagination inside.[1]

When I was much younger and more prone to be incensed by injustice than I am now, I was invited by a small college in Northern California to be on a panel as part of their "Indian Awareness Week." There was a "Black Awareness Week" and a "Chicano Awareness Week," which left, if I've done the math correctly, forty-nine "White Awareness Weeks." Still, it was a chance to say something meaningful, and being politically naive and eager, I accepted.

There were four of us: a Mohawk artist, two guys from the Bureau of Indian Affairs, and me. The Mohawk guy talked eloquently about traditional art, spirituality, and pride. The two guys from Washington made pragmatic speeches complete with charts and overheads to show the kinds of programs that were available to Native people who wished to better themselves, along with the kinds of economic opportunities that various government agencies were providing for the benefit of tribes, such as oil exploration, coal mining, dam construction, clear-cut logging ventures, and nuclear waste storage.

For my part, I told stories. Stories about broken treaties, residential schools, culturally offensive movies, the appropriation of Native names, symbols, and motifs.

And Ishi.

It's a famous story and I imagine some of you know it. Or know a few of the details. And then again, maybe you don't.

In the summer of 1911, near the town of Oroville in Northern California, butchers found an Indian behind a slaughterhouse. He was, not to put too fine a point on it, a surprise. Indians in this part of the world had been persecuted for years. Gold miners, landowners, and your average God-fearing gun-loving enthusiasts such as the group of White men who massacred the Wiyots off the coast of Northern California in 1860, had forced Native peoples out of their homes, and in many instances, simply hunted them down and shot them on sight. More than likely, the people in Oroville didn't know there were any Indians left in the area.

This one was not in particularly good shape. He was sick, hungry, and near death. The butchers called the sheriff, and the sheriff, not knowing what to do with him, put him in a cell reserved for the insane at the local jail.

The papers called him the "Wild Man of Oroville."

He was a Yahi. Maybe part Maidu. Maybe part Wintu. No one really knows. But like James Fenimore Cooper's Chingachgook, and Peter Such's Shawnadithit, he appeared to be the last of his people. Had he died in jail, there wouldn't have been much of a story.

But he didn't.

He was rescued — and I use the word "rescued" guardedly — by Alfred L. Kroeber and Thomas Talbot Waterman, two anthropologists from the newly opened Anthropological Museum at the University of California in San Francisco. With the co-operation and permission of the Bureau of Indian Affairs, who believed that they owned all Native people in U.S. America, Kroeber and Waterman took the Wild Man of Oroville to San Francisco and gave him a place to stay at the museum.

His name wasn't Ishi. He never told anyone his name. Kroeber, under pressure from reporters who got tired of calling the Indian the Wild Man of Oroville, named him Ishi, a Yahi word that means simply "man." For the next five years, until his death in 1916 from tuberculosis, Ishi lived and worked at the museum.

He was even given a job. Junior janitor. Twenty-five dollars a month plus, of course, room and board. It wasn't a bad life, and Ishi, from all accounts, enjoyed it. He had the freedom to come and go as he pleased. He rode the trolley cars in San Francisco, went to the opera and the ocean. He followed doctors as they made their rounds at the university hospital. He was fascinated, according to Theodora Kroeber, not so much by what Whites did as by their numbers. And each Sunday afternoon, for about two and a half hours, he demonstrated Indian arts and crafts — arrow making, hide preparation — for the curious of the city. He was not, so far as we know, abused. Kroeber kept the vultures away, refusing the requests to put Ishi on the vaudeville circuit or in the circus. There were no "I Saw Ishi" T-shirts, no boxes of Ishi breakfast cereal, no Upper Deck Ishi rookie cards, and no bobble head Ishi dolls.

The people at the museum were inordinately fond of pointing out that Ishi was, in fact, free to return to the mountains and lava fields of Northern California if he chose to do so.

You can go home any time you wish, they told him.

Which must have made him laugh and cry at the same time.

For there was no home. No family. Not anymore. Ishi hadn't come out of the mountains because he had seen an advertisement in the employment section of a newspaper.

"Help wanted. Museum curiosity. Apply in person."

He had to come to that slaughterhouse to escape the killings and the loneliness, and he would stay at the museum until his own death because he had nowhere else to go.

It's a killer story, isn't it. And I told it with vigour. I probably waved my hands, raised my voice, may have even banged the podium. And when it was all over, after the guys in their suits had packed up their charts and transparencies and sat down, it was clear that the Indians had carried the day. You could see it in the eyes of the audience. Some of the women were actually crying. And what applause!

As we filed off the stage, one of the organizers, the woman who had invited me to speak, appeared. She shook hands with each of the guys from Washington, and at the same time handed them an envelope. I was delighted. I knew what was in that envelope.

An honorarium.

I nudged the Mohawk guy, but he had already seen the envelopes. I must admit I had my money spent before I even got to the woman. She shook my hand and thanked me for coming and told me that she thought my remarks would stay with her for a long time. But she didn't give me an envelope. For a moment I thought she had forgotten.

So I held on to her hand. She could have it back when I got my envelope.

But there was no envelope, and the woman seemed surprised I even asked.

Were you promised money? she wanted to know.

Well, no, we hadn't been promised any money, I said, but you paid the other guys.

That's true, she told me, her tone suggesting that she didn't quite understand my complaint. But, after all, she said, they're the experts.

What were we, I wanted to know, entertainment?

It was a rhetorical question. The woman was supposed to be embarrassed and apologize. She was supposed to promise to find the necessary funds to pay us for our time.

But she didn't.

There were other invitations. So many, in fact, that my loose collection of sound and fury quickly coalesced into a rather polished and potent presentation, and, as I wandered from campus to campus, I became, God help me, a Spokesperson.

Special, tonight only.

Return of the Complaining Native.

Hear It from a Real Indian.

White Depredations. Indian Deprivations.

You'll laugh, you'll cry.

Wine and cheese reception to follow.

Entertainment. Probably not as much fun as being tossed around, say, on a mechanical bull or watching a good hockey fight on Friday night, but several steps up from bowling.

At first I thought it was just me. That in my haste to make a difference, in my desire to change the world, I had become a caricature of protest. So I toned down my indignation, did some historical research so I could throw out the occasional date, turned in my ribbon shirt, my four-strand bone choker, and my beaded belt buckle for a cheap but serviceable suit and a rather nice tie, and arrived at the next confrontation virtually indistinguishable from the boys from Washington.

At the end of that presentation, which I thought went rather well, a young Native man about my age, dressed in a ribbon shirt, bone choker, and beaded belt buckle, the very markers of race that I had so casually abandoned, stood up and asked me what the hell an "apple" was doing speaking for real Indians. For those of you who do not know what an "apple" is, it's a derogatory term for an Indian who is red on the outside and white on the inside. An Uncle Tomahawk, if you will. In the 1960s and 1970s, it was the worst insult you could hurl at another Indian.

Needless to say, I was hurt.

But worse, there was that rhetorical question again. As long as I dressed like an Indian and complained like an Indian, I was entertainment. But if I dressed like a non-Indian and reasoned like a non-Indian, then not only was I not entertainment, I wasn't an Indian.

Stay with me.

Therefore, if I dressed like an Indian and acted like an Indian — and here it would help if you've seen the witch skit in *Monty Python and the Holy Grail* — I must be . . . entertainment.

Most of you are probably waiting for the sting, where I turn this conceit back on itself and say something profound or at least clever. But, as it turns out, I have nowhere to go.

What am I?

Entertainment.

Actually, as it turns out, it's not just me. It's Indians in general. Somewhere along the way, we ceased being people and somehow became performers in an Aboriginal minstrel show for White North America.

But we didn't begin that way. We haven't always been entertainment. Once upon a time, we were . . . other things.

I've always been a reader. Sometimes out of interest. Sometimes out of necessity. Sometimes to get out of the heat. I was raised in the Sacramento Valley of California, and during the summers the temperature would climb to forty degrees Celsius and above. The house we lived in did not have air conditioning, and the only cool place in the entire town that did not charge an admission fee was the library. The library wasn't air conditioned, either, but it had a basement that was cool and walls that were stacked with books.

I was fond of adventure fiction, but my favourite stories were about the discovery, exploration, and settlement of the Americas: William Prescott's *History of the Conquest of Mexico* and *History of the Conquest of Peru*, for example. The epic adventures of empire. Men with swords. Men with flags. Men with Bibles.

And Indians.

Well, not Indians exactly. And not entertainment either. At least not yet.

Most historians mark the beginning of Indian-European contact with Columbus wading ashore somewhere in the Caribbean, striding up the beach, flag in hand, and taking possession of the land and all that was there for the king and queen of Spain on October 12, 1492. We know now that Vikings had landed in North America some four or five hundred years earlier, but the tenth-century settlements at L'Anse aux Meadows in Newfoundland had a short tenure, whereas Columbus's arrival marked the beginning of a permanent European presence in the

Americas. And the beginning of the stories that Europeans would tell about Native peoples.

"These people are very poor in everything," Columbus is supposed to have written in his journal. "They all go quite naked as their mothers bore them. . . . They bear no arms, no know thereof; for I showed them swords and they grasped them by the blade and cut themselves through ignorance. . . . They are generally fairly tall and good-looking, well built. . . . They ought to be good servants and of good skill, for I see that they repeat very quickly whatever was said to them. I believe that they would easily be made Christians, because it seemed to me that they belonged to no religion."[2]

Nothing wrong with this. Columbus didn't know where he was. He didn't know who the people were. So he guessed. Since he was looking for India, these must be Indians. Not his fault he was lost. And for all the erroneous assumptions that this first description contains, it's a reasonably honest report of what the good admiral saw. Tall, good-looking, naked people who were unfamiliar with steel weapons.

We can forgive and forget the nonsense about being "good servants" and the "easily be made into Christians" part, can't we? That was just wishful thinking.

Explorers who came after Columbus would describe Native people in much the same way. Pedro Vaz de Caminha, who sailed with Pedro Álvares Cabral for Brazil in 1500, wrote a letter to King Manuel of Portugal in which he described the Tupinambá Indians as having good faces and noses. "They go naked," Caminha told the king, "neither do they pay more attention to concealing or exposing their shame than they do to showing their faces, and in this respect they are very innocent."[3]

In 1505, Gaspar Corte Real kidnapped approximately fifty Indians, men and women, from the coast of Newfoundland and sent them back to Spain to be examined by Alberto Cantino. They were much like Europeans, Cantino conceded, "their speech is unintelligible, but nevertheless is not harsh but rather human. Their manners and gestures are most gentle; they laugh considerably and manifest the greatest pleasure."[4]

Through most of the sixteenth and early seventeenth centuries, explorers such as Giovanni da Verrazzano, Jacques Cartier, Francis Drake, Martin Frobisher, Arthur Barlowe, John Brereton, and James Rosier visited the Americas and sent back reports of Indians who were civil, good looking, gentle, quick witted, and, of course, naked.

But along with these good reports, many of which played off some of the ideas that Europeans had of Western mythologies such as Eden and Atlantis, were less savoury descriptions of Indians. Amerigo Vespucci, who may never have made it to the Americas at all, described Indians as indecent, immoral, and cannibalistic. Sir Francis Drake, who found the Indians of California loving and without guile or treachery, was concerned about the influence that the Devil had over these simple people. Jacques Cartier, who had been well treated by the Indians of the St. Lawrence River region, complained that they were great thieves, an ironic complaint, to be sure, for the historian who knows that Cartier capped off his second voyage by kidnapping ten Indians and taking them back to France with him.

Though we shouldn't think that poorly of Jacques. Everyone did it. Taking Indians as souvenirs, it seems, was an explorer's prerogative. Columbus took ten Indians back with him on his first voyage and, on his second, rounded up Indians en masse, five hundred at a time, and shipped them back to Seville to be sold in the slave markets.

A number of years back, I wrote a children's book called *A Coyote Columbus Story* in which I suggested that it was that ubiquitous Native trickster Coyote who created Columbus and his crew, so Coyote would have someone with whom he could play baseball. Things didn't work out exactly as Coyote had planned them, which is typical, and, in the end, Columbus tells Coyote to stuff his baseball game, has his men round up as many Indians as the ships will hold, and sends them back to Spain to be sold as slaves.

One annoyed reviewer complained that, while imagination was a good thing in children's literature, I should not be inventing history in order to make a political point. She was, it turned out, angry about my suggesting that Columbus had enslaved Indians. And when I told her that this was the only part of my story that was accurate, she refused to believe me.

I wasn't trying to ruin Columbus's good name, but somebody had to pay for these voyages. Sailing the ocean blue was expensive, and slavery was a brisk and profitable business. If Africans made good slaves — and here we have to ignore the pernicious assumptions on which that statement is based — why not give Indians a try? You can see the logic. Unfortunately Indians who were sent to the slave markets had the annoying habit of dying before they could be auctioned off, and the enterprise was soon abandoned.

Besides, Indians were a much more valuable resource to explorers. Particularly when it came to the question of what was where, and as long as Europeans were strangers in a strange land, Indians, innocent, deceitful, and naked though they may have been, were the only guides to this new world that explorers had.

Can't find the Seven Cities of Gold? Ask an Indian.

Looking for the Fountain of Youth? Ask an Indian.

Need to find a water route to the Orient? Ask an Indian.

Living together would be another matter, and, as exploration gave way to settlement, the European reaction to Indians hardened, and the language used to describe Indians intensified. Particularly among the English. While the Spanish depended on Indians as a slave labour force to work the mines and plantations in New Spain, the British and the French depended on the Indians as partners in the fur trade, and then as an adjunct mercenary force so they could fight each other, and later, of course, the Americans. But apart from these specific roles, none of these nations had much use for Indians.

This was particularly true of the Puritans in New England, who had brought with them a religion that was militaristic in nature and a theory of land acquisition and usage that was individualistic and private. Thanksgiving and corn-planting techniques aside, Indians were, most often, seen as impediments to progress and affronts to faith.

You might be wondering why I'm about to use an American example to discuss early Native–non-Native relations instead of a good Canadian example. I could say that it's because I'd prefer to put the Americans on the spot and pretend that Canadians treated Indians better. But that's not true. It's because I know the American example better, and because Americans started the process of eliminating Indians sooner and were more diligent about the project than were Canadians.

Don't worry, my partner, who is a staunch Canadian, has already had words with me about this rather lame bit of reasoning.

So the Puritans saw the world at war, a holy war, a war that was both philosophical and physical. Philosophically, God and the Devil were engaged in a spiritual battle for the souls of humans. Humans, in turn, fought a physical battle that pitted God's troops, in this case the Puritans, against the Devil's mercenaries. While they were in England, the Puritans had seen the manifestations of the Devil in the pomp of the Catholic church and in the impurity of the Anglican order. Transplanting themselves to America did not take them out of the battle. It simply pitted them against an old enemy in a new guise.

Land, on the other hand, was a godsend, satisfying two needs for the Puritans. First, it provided them the space in which to establish a community, something they had not had in land-poor England. Second, it provided settlers with enough room to isolate their community, so that the worldly influences that had plagued them in England could be walled out, and the forces of darkness and the wilderness could be kept at bay.

Indians were seen as a threat both to the war effort and to the acquisition of land, and the Puritans set about creating the stories that were needed to carry the day. Indians, who had been imagined as strange and exotic in the halcyon days of exploration, were now seen, as the historian Douglas Edward Leach put it, a "graceless and savage people, dirty and slothful in their personal habits, treacherous in their relations with the superior race . . . fit only to be pushed aside and subordinated."[5]

William Morrell, in his terse verse history of New England, imagined Native people as dangerous. "They're wonderous cruel," he wrote, "Strangely base and vile/Quickly displeased, and hardly reconciled."[6] Nathanial Saltonstall, writing of King Philip's War in New England, 1675–76, likened Indians to wolves "and other beasts of prey that commonly do their mischiefs in the night or by stealth durst not come forth out of the woods and swamps where they lay skulking in small companies."[7]

And when they did come out of the woods and swamps, according to Benjamin Trumbull, they ate each other. Of a captive, Trumbull writes, "The Indians, kindling a large fire, violently tore him limb from limb. Barbarously cutting his flesh in pieces, they handed it round from one to another, eating it, singing and dancing round the fire, in their violent and tumultuous manner."[8]

These descriptions, these historical propagandas, made their way into a great many historical fictions, the best of which is probably John Richardson's 1852 novel *Wau-Nan-Gee, or, The Massacre at Chicago*. In it, Richardson — a Canadian, for those of you who share my partner's nationalistic tendencies — describes a group of Potawatomies, led by the arch-villain Pee-to-tum, who have just attacked a wagon. It's a sparkling passage, full of the balance and sensitivity that marks the best of Hollywood westerns.

"Squatted in a circle, and within a few feet of the wagon in which the tomahawked children lay covered with blood, and fast stiffening in the coldness of death, now sat about twenty Indians, with Pee-to-tum at their head, passing from hand to hand the quivering heart of the slain man, whose eyes, straining as it were, from their sockets, seemed to watch the horrid repast in which they were indulging, while the blood streamed disgustingly over their chins and lips and trickled over their persons. So many wolves or tigers could not have torn away more voraciously with their teeth, or smacked their lips with greater delight in the relish of human food, than did these loathsome creatures who now moistened the nauseous repast from a black bottle of rum which had been found in one of the wagons containing the medicine for the sick — and what gave additional disgust was the hideous aspect of the inflamed eye of the Chippewa, from which the bandage had fallen off, and from which the heat of the sun's rays was fast drawing a briny, ropy, and copious discharge, resembling rather the grey and slimy mucus of the toad than the tears of a human being."[9]

Yummy.

All that in two sentences.

Indians, it seemed, could offer little inspiration or example to civilized humans, and colonists saw little need to examine either the Indian or Indian culture. Indian government was a labyrinth, confused and indecipherable. Indian religion was absurd and ridiculous. Jonas Johannis Michaluis, in a letter to the Reverend Adrianus Smoutuis, summed up the feelings that most colonists had for Indians when he described them as "savage and wild, strangers to all decency, yea, uncivil and stupid as garden poles."[10]

"Stupid as garden poles." It's funny, isn't it? And a little annoying, too. But there's no point in being angry. These are just the sounds and smells of empire — fear, racism, greed, arrogance — and since empire tends to be exclusive, it makes sense, doesn't it, that Indians would not be welcome?

I fear that this is beginning to sound like one of those boring litany of complaints about the past. You know, Native peoples as hapless victims, innocents in the struggle for the Americas.

Well, shame on me.

We understand, do we not, that we can't judge the past by the standards of the present? And we agree, don't we, that a religion should not be measured by the actions of the people who profess to practise it? And we've told ourselves enough times, in one form or another, that the sins of the father — gender biases notwithstanding — should not be visited on the son.

Of course, the skeptic would point out that these axioms are little more than self-serving attempts to insure ourselves against liability, that many of our past peccadilloes — African slavery, for example — were known to be wrong at the time we committed them, while the cynic would argue that the lessons of history only serve to show us which atrocities are profitable and which are not.

But not me. Complaint is not my purpose. This little history lesson is simply my attempt to call attention to the cultural distance that separated Europeans and Indians. We don't know, for example, if there were many Indians who wanted to be Europeans, but we do know that Europeans, as a group, had little interest in being Indians. The Spanish were dead against it, the French may have lived with Indians and married Indians but that was primarily in the cause of the fur trade, and the Puritans saw any inclinations toward the forest and Aboriginal life as proof of an unsound mind and the Devil's handiwork, the terror of which is so pleasantly captured in Nathaniel Hawthorne's short story "Young Goodman Brown."

But in the second half of the nineteenth century a strange thing happened in North America. After three centuries of trying to eradicate Indians, Europeans suddenly became interested in Indians. Not all Europeans, of course. Mostly those who lived east of the Mississippi, or in Ontario and Quebec, those who had never seen an Indian, those for whom Indians were a distant memory.

Not out in the West, where Indians were still a reality and where, on occasion, they could still be an annoyance, even dangerous.

And not just any Indian.

Not the Indian who had been assimilated to the plow. Not the Indian who had been crippled by European diseases and vices. Not the Indian who had been buried on reservations and locked up in military prisons. Certainly not the educated Indian who had fought American expansion in the courts. Rather it was the wild, free, powerful, noble, handsome, philosophical, eloquent, solitary Indian — pardon me, solitary male Indian — that Europeans went looking to find. A particular Indian. An Indian who could be a cultural treasure, a piece of North American antiquity. A mythic figure who could reflect the strength and freedom of an emerging continent.

A National Indian.

Within the North American imagination, Native people have always been an exotic, erotic, terrifying presence. Much like the vast tracts of wilderness that early explorers and settlers faced. But most of all, Native people have been confusing. The panorama of cultures, the innumerable tribes, and the complex of languages made it impossible for North Americans to find what they most desired.

A single Indian who could stand for the whole.

But if North Americans couldn't find him, they could make him up. In fact, without knowing it, they had been working on this very project almost from first contact.

In 1734, the king's surveyor general and assistant

governor for the state of New Hampshire, David Dunbar, sent a small party of men to the village of Exeter to enforce the crown's Mast Tree law. This was a law that allowed the crown to claim any trees that were suitable to be turned into masts for the Royal Navy. Public trees, private trees, it didn't matter. If it could be turned into a serviceable mast, it belonged to the king. Needless to say, this was not a particularly popular law among the colonists, and, when Dunbar's party settled down for the night and were enjoying their evening meal at a local inn, they were suddenly attacked by Indians.

Well, not exactly Indians. Whites dressed up like Indians. Blankets, feathers, painted faces, war clubs. Lots of snarling and whooping and howling as they attacked Dunbar's men and chased them out of town.

In 1773, a war party of Mohawks ran through the streets of Boston on their way to a ship that was anchored in the harbour. The Mohawks boarded the *Dartmouth* and spent the next three hours throwing the ship's cargo overboard. This was, of course, the famous Boston Tea Party, and the Indians were, once again, not Indians but Whites, disgusted by the tax that the crown had placed on tea and determined to show their displeasure by dressing up like Indians and dumping the tea into the bay.

Neither of these incidents had much to do with Indians. They were both about civil disobedience. And in neither case were the participants trying to disguise their identities. Everyone knew the perpetrators weren't Indians. So why dress up like Indians? Why not dress up like British soldiers or Portuguese fishermen or Jesuits?

Why not just wear masks or hoods? Why bother dressing up at all?

The Lakota scholar Philip Deloria, in his critical study *Playing Indian*, suggests that these guises were a rhetorical device, that "Indianness helped the Mast Tree rioters [and the Boston Tea Party participants as well] define custom and imagine themselves a legitimate part of the continent's ancient history. Indians and the land," Deloria argues, "offered the only North American past capable of justifying a claim of traditional custom and a refiguring of the rhetoric of moral economy. Native people had been on the land for centuries, and they embodied a full complement of the necessary traditions. By becoming Indian, New Hampshirites sought to appropriate those laws of custom. White Indians laid claim, not to real Indian practices, of course, but to the idea of native custom. . . . the specifics to be defined not by Indians, but by colonists."[11]

At the same time that eighteenth-century colonists in the countryside were dressing up like Indians to dramatize economic and political grievances, more metropolitan and affluent fraternal organizations, such as the Tammany society, the society of Red Men, and the Improved Order of Red Men, were using the idea of the Indian to anchor their order to an American antiquity. Like their rowdier country cousins, lodge members dressed up like real Indians, not as an occasion for complaint but as an occasion for celebration. Members painted their faces like real Indians, walked in single file like real Indians, carried bows and arrows like real Indians, smoked the peace pipe like real Indians, were given Indian names like real Indians, engaged in initiation ceremonies like real Indians, had secret handshakes and codes and signs like real Indians, and even talked like real Indians.

Nobody wanted to be Grey Owl quite yet. That would come later.

At the same time, real Indians were being obstinate. In the northeast, Native leaders such as the Miami Little Turtle, the Mohawk Joseph Brant, and the Shawnee Blue Jacket began forming coalitions to resist American expansion into their territory, while, in the southeast, the Cherokees, Creeks, Choctaws, and Chickasaws, unable to get the American government to live up to the terms of the Hopewell Treaties, began attacking pioneer outposts. From the 1780s until after the War of 1812, warriors from various tribes fought on their own and with the British against the Americans.

Which made the matter of playing Indian problematic. But not impossible. After all, the constructed Indians dancing and smoking, walking around single file, whispering passwords to one another, and exchanging secret handshakes in the comfort of a panelled clubhouse had little to do with the other constructed Indians skulking about in a forest. And by the middle of the eighteenth century, the one had virtually replaced the other.

Well, "replaced" is probably too sweeping a term. Let's just say that a pattern began to emerge that would create a singular semi-historic Indian who was a friend to the White man, who was strong, brave, honest, and noble. A figure who kept his clothes on and who spoke reasonable English.

Such a figure was certainly needed. After all, according to popular perception, Indians were dying. Everywhere you looked Indians were vanishing, swept away by disease, war, and the advance of civilization. Not a thing anyone could do about it, of course, simply the workings of a natural law that decreed that superior cultures should displace inferior cultures.

The Reverend John Heckewelder, a Moravian missionary to the Delaware Indians, in his 1818 *Account of the History, Manners, and Customs of the Indian Nations Who Once Inhabited Pennsylvania and the Neighboring States*, articulated this sentiment when he lamented that "in a few year perhaps, they [Indians] will have entirely disappeared from the face of the earth, and all that will be remembered of them will be that they existed and were numbered among the barbarous tribes that once inhabited this vast Continent."[12]

The painter George Catlin, on his travels through North America, saw the Indian and the buffalo as fugitives from civilization. "They have fled," said Catlin, "to the great plains of the West, and there under an equal doom, they have taken up their last abode, where their race will expire and their bones will bleach together."[13]

General Sanborn, in a speech on Indian education, closed on a particularly dismal note, echoing the common convictions of a nation on the move. "Little can be hoped for them [Indians] as a distinct people," he proffered. "The sun of their day is fast sinking in the western sky. It will soon go down in a night of oblivion that shall know no morning. . . . No spring-time shall renew their fading glory, and no future know their fame,"[14] while Horace Greeley, on a trip to the West in 1859, left sentiment and purple prose behind. "The Indians are children," Greely bluntly declared, "their arts, wars, treaties, alliances, habitations, crafts, properties, commerce, comforts, all belong to the very lowest and rudest of human existence. . . . I could not help saying, 'These people must die out — there is no help for them.'"[15]

Great stuff. And potent. So potent, in fact, that not only did these wishful fictions convince Whites of the imminent demise of Native peoples, but they also persuaded many Native people that they had no future as Indians.

Indians such as Charles Eastman.

Eastman was Lakota, one of the more famous Indians of his day. He had been raised traditionally on the Canadian prairies and then at age fifteen was sent off to a series of schools by his father, Many Lightnings, who was convinced that Christianity and White culture were the wave of the future. Eastman's education took him to the Santee Agency school in Santee, Nebraska, and from there to Beloit College in Wisconsin, to Dartmouth, and on to Boston College, where he earned a medical degree. He served as the physician at the Pine Ridge Agency in the winter of 1890 when the Seventh Cavalry massacred Big Foot's band at Wounded Knee Creek, and went on to write — with the strong assistance of his wife, Elaine Goodall Eastman — eleven books, several of which — *Indian Boyhood* (1902), *The Soul of the Indian* (1911), and *From the Deep Woods to Civilization* (1921) —

were about traditional Indian life and Eastman's experiences with the non-Native world. And while he saw the inherent faults in White civilization ("I have wondered much," Eastman wrote in *From the Deep Woods to Civilization*, "that Christianity is not practiced by the very people who vouch for that wonderful conception of exemplary living. It appears that they are anxious to pass on their religion to all races of men, but keep very little of it themselves"),[16] he was, in the end, convinced that there was no chance for Indians to maintain their former, simple lives, that they would either have to assimilate or die. "I am an Indian," Eastman declared in the closing paragraph of the book, "and while I have learned much from civilization, for which I am grateful, I have never lost my Indian sense of right and justice. . . . Nevertheless, so long as I live, I am an American."[17]

But who exactly was this Indian Eastman believed himself to be, and who exactly was this American he believed he had become?

While Charles Eastman was making his way from the deep woods to civilization, E. Pauline Johnson was making her way from the Mohawk reserve at Six Nations (near Brantford, Ontario) to the stage and the lectern. A mixed-blood like Eastman, Johnson was best known for her poetry performances that played to sell-out crowds in Canada and England. Dressed for the first half of the program in a composite/makeshift, semi-traditional Native-inspired outfit complete with fur pelts, wampum belts, her father's hunting knife, and a scalp she was given by a Blackfoot chief, Johnson would then switch to an elegant evening gown for the second half, providing the audience with the Native exoticism they craved and the English sophistication they trusted.

On occasion, Johnson would reverse the order of the costumes and do the first half of her performance in a gown, only then switching to her Native outfit. But this was not as popular because it inverted and challenged the idea of order and progress that Western civilization had decreed and that her audiences expected.

And desired.

Both Eastman and Johnson were performers, though Johnson arguably realized it more completely than did Eastman. Eastman, if we can trust the sentiment in his books, was searching for a way to explain the dichotomy between Christian theory and Christian practice, while Johnson was looking for a way to make a living. Delightfully, her business card read, "Pauline Johnson, Mohawk Author — Entertainer."

The success that both Eastman and Johnson had at the turn of the century depended, in large part, on their Native pedigree. Eastman's origins as a "wild" Indian were a never-ending source of fascination for his White audiences, while Johnson's connection to "Mohawk royalty" (her father and grandfather were major figures at Six Nations) provided her with equally intriguing credentials. Neither Eastman nor Johnson, though, could match a figure such as Sitting Bull, who, nine years after the Battle of the Little Bighorn, was touring with Buffalo Bill's Wild West Show at a salary of $50 a week, plus a $150 signing bonus. Nor were these examples the exceptions.

Gabriel Dumont toured with Buffalo Bill. So did Black Elk. So did about thirty Indians who had been involved in the 1890 Wounded Knee Massacre. Seen as malcontents, they were given the choice of touring with Buffalo Bill or going to jail.

An easy choice, if you ask me.

At least they had a choice. Fifteen years earlier, in 1875, seventy-two Kiowas, Comanches, Cheyennes, and Arapahoes were rounded up and sent to prison at Fort Marion in Florida for no better reason than they were Indian. To alleviate the boredom, the Indians were given ledger books and coloured pencils and encouraged to draw. Considered curiosities rather than art, these drawings became a kind of currency in the travel game, and many a tourist stopped by the fort to see the Indians dance and draw and to purchase a memento of the visit.

And let's not forget Ishi.

If we were given to creating categories in order to organize the world, we might be tempted to divide turn-of-the-century Indians into two groups. The first might be the "wild" Indian — Crazy Horse, for example — who refused the gifts of civilization, never made peace, and remained an unrepentant warrior to his death, while the second could be the educated Indian, an Indian — such as Charles Eastman — who saw in White culture the only future that was available to Native people.

Of course, nothing is quite so simple.

Though we would like it to be. Several years ago, John Stackhouse, a reporter for the *Globe and Mail*, came to Winnipeg to do a story on the *Dead Dog Café*, a Native radio show that ran on CBC for about five years. The *Dead Dog Café* gang — Edna Rain, Floyd Favell Starr, and myself — were in town to do a *Dead Dog Café* special. Stackhouse talked to each of us, watched the show, and went back to Toronto to write his story, which turned out to be a curious piece that was as much about the different categories of Indians — authentic and inauthentic — as it was about the show itself.

Edna, according to the article, was the most authentic Indian in the cast, "the show's . . . truest aboriginal person in terms of her life's experience," Stackhouse wrote. "On weekends, she returns to her reserve to skin, smoke and tan animal hides, and chop wood. . . . She once showed up for rehearsal with a dead moose in her trunk."[18]

Floyd, on the other hand, is a kind of transitional figure, splitting his time between the Poundmaker reserve, where he was born and raised, and the urbanity of Winnipeg's theatre world. "He participates in ceremonies such as sweats and listens to hard-rock music stations,"[19] Stackhouse observed.

I'm the urban Indian. Not an Indian at all, really. "A bundle of contradictions," Stackhouse called me, "equal parts first class and first nations."[20] My sins include insisting on flying business class, playing golf with Graham Greene, owning a big house in Guelph, having three cats, and vacationing in Costa Rica.

And then there's my "floral golf shirt."

Remember that four-strand bone choker and beaded belt buckle that I so foolishly gave up?

Actually, Stackhouse was wrong about me. I have two

cats, not three. Oh, and it wasn't a dead moose in Edna's trunk, it was a tanned moose hide. Any self-indulgent urban Indian who golfs with Graham Greene knows that not even the Mercedes S 500 could hold an animal that large.

Stackhouse's article appeared under the banner "Comic Heroes or 'Red Niggers'?" and appropriates once again the old question of who is being entertainment and for whom. Comic heroes for Natives and "Red Niggers" for Whites? Or is it comic heroes for Whites and "Red Niggers" for Natives? And is it possible for us to move past this limiting dichotomy?

Charles Eastman and Pauline Johnson entertained White audiences. Did they entertain other Natives? Sure. Did they entertain themselves? One would hope so.

What about Ishi? He didn't have any Native people to entertain. There were just the non-Natives who surrounded him. And himself.

Strange world. But maybe being entertainment isn't so bad. Maybe it's what you're left with when the only defence you have is a good story. Maybe entertainment is the story of survival.

Take Ishi's story, for example. It's yours. Do with it what you will. Put Ishi's face on a T-shirt. Drive up to Oroville and visit the site of the slaughterhouse. Forget it. But don't say in the years to come that you would have lived your life differently if only you had heard this story.

You've heard it now.

IV

A MILLION PORCUPINES
CRYING IN THE DARK

THERE IS A STORY I KNOW. It's about the earth and how it floats in space on the back of a turtle. I've heard this story many times, and each time someone tells the story, it changes. Sometimes the change is simply in the voice of the storyteller. Sometimes the change is in the details. Sometimes in the order of events. Other times it's the dialogue or the response of the audience. But in all the tellings of all the tellers, the world never leaves the turtle's back. And the turtle never swims away.

One time, it was in Trois-Rivières I think, a man in the audience who was taking notes asked about the turtle and the earth. If the earth was on the back of a turtle, what was below the turtle? Another turtle, the storyteller told him. And below that turtle? Another turtle. And below that? Another turtle.

The man quickly scribbled down notes, enjoying the game, I imagine. So how many turtles are there? he wanted to know. The storyteller shrugged. No one knows for sure, she told him, but it's turtles all the way down.

The truth about stories is that that's all we are. "I will tell you something about stories," the Laguna storyteller Leslie Silko reminds us, "They aren't just entertainment/Don't be fooled/They are all we have, you see/All we have to fight off/Illness and death. You don't have anything/If you don't have the stories."[1]

Over the years, I've lost more than my fair share of friends to suicide. The majority of them have been mixed-bloods. Native men and women who occupied those racial shadow zones that have been created for us and that we create for ourselves. The latest and greatest loss was the Choctaw-Cherokee-Irish writer Louis Owens, who killed himself in an airport parking garage on his way to an academic conference in Bellingham, Washington.

Louis was a fine novelist and an even better literary/cultural critic and theorist. But most especially, he was a good friend, more a brother, really. We were of a like age, shared much the same background, were haunted by the same fears. We loved fly-fishing and the solitude of quiet places. We understood in each other the same desperate desire for acceptance. And we were both hopeful pessimists. That is, we wrote knowing that none of the stories we told would change the world. But we wrote in the hope that they would.

We both knew that stories were medicine, that a story told one way could cure, that the same story told another way could injure. In his memoir *I Hear the Train*, Louis tells the story of a summer that he spent picking tomatoes. It was 1965. The year before, the U.S. government had decided to end the Bracero program that had brought half a million migrant workers up from Mexico each year to work in the fields of California. Faced with the continuing need for cheap labour and the prospect of a long, hot, politically dangerous summer — urban riots, Vietnam protests, and disillusioned youth had been the order of business the summer before — politicians at the state capitol came up with the bright idea of making field jobs — normally the domain of Mexican workers — available to Blacks from the inner cities and to the generic poor.

"The government men decided to call it an economic opportunity work program," Louis writes. "Any lucky person with a sufficiently low income, they announced, could qualify to work in the fields for minimum wage. They advertised the program heavily and recruited in Los Angeles, Stockton, Compton, East Palo Alto, Oakland — those places where summer jobs for Black teens had never existed and where young Black males with time on their hands posed potential complications for the coming summer. Somehow we heard about it in Atascadero. It sounded like fun."[2]

The labour camp where the workers were required to stay was an old military barracks left over from World War II that, over the years, had housed thousands of Mexican workers. Now it housed close to three hundred young Black men and a handful of others. The barracks where the workers stayed were spartan at best. Old metal cots lined both sides of a long, narrow room, with mattresses flattened thin and hard as plywood by seasons of exhausted farm workers.

Best of all, a new ten-foot chain-link fence had been thrown up around the camp, topped with barbed wire to make sure no one wandered away. Each night the camp was locked and a guard stationed at the gate. Each morning Louis and the other workers were let out and taken to the fields. Each evening they were brought back and locked up again.

It was hard work. The food that was provided was inedible. Worse, the workers were charged for it. As well they were charged for their cots, for transportation to and from the fields, for insurance, and for anything else the growers could think up. And when the first payday rolled around, after all the expenses had been deducted, Louis discovered that he had spent more money than he had made. Twelve dollars to be exact.

This experiment in economic opportunity didn't last long. Three weeks. Given the rate at which the workers were going broke, it probably wouldn't have lasted much longer anyway, but halfway through the third week, a White mob from the nearby town of Merced attacked the camp with the intention of burning it down. The police held the mob off, and it contented itself with turning cars over and setting them on fire. Louis and the rest of the men stayed inside the fence, armed with metal cot legs and makeshift knives, waiting for the big fight.

But it never happened.

The mob eventually dispersed, and, in the morning, the workers came into the yard to find the front gate wide

open, the supervisors and the guard gone. No trucks
came to pick them up that day, and, by afternoon, everyone began the long walk home. For many, that walk was
over three hundred miles, with little chance of catching a
ride with a passing motorist.

In *I Hear the Train*, Louis recalls that moment and won-
ders, "[W]here are those fellows today, the ones I picked
tomatoes and played basketball and watched a mob
with? Do they sit in midlife and wonder, as I do, whether
it really happened at all? Whether their memories, like
mine, are warped and shadowed far beyond reliability.
Whether even trying to put such a thing into words is an
absurd endeavor, as if such things are best left to turn and
drift in inarticulate memory like those river pebbles that
get worn more and more smooth over time until there are
no edges."[3]

Maybe this was the story Louis told himself as he sat
in that airport garage. A story about poor young men
walking home alone. Maybe it was another. Whichever
one it was, for that instant Louis must have believed it.

Did you ever wonder how it is we imagine the world in
the way we do, how it is we imagine ourselves, if not
through our stories. And in the English-speaking world,
nothing could be easier, for we are surrounded by stories,
and we can trace these stories back to other stories and
from there back to the beginnings of language. For these
are our stories, the cornerstones of our culture.

You all know the names. Masculine names that grace
the tables of contents of the best anthologies, all neatly

arranged chronologically so we can watch the march of literary progress. A cumulative exercise in the early years, it has broadened its empire in the last few decades, sending scouting parties into new territory to find new voices. These days, English literature anthologies contain the works of women writers, Black writers, Hispanic writers, Asian writers, gay and lesbian writers, and, believe it or not, a few Native writers.

All in the cause of culture, all in the service of literacy, which we believe to be an essential skill. Indeed, the ability to read and write and keep records is understood as one of the primary markers of an advanced civilization. One of my professors at university argued that you could not have a "dependable" literature without literacy, that the two went hand in hand.

I'm sure he would have been buoyed by Statistics Canada's figures of Canadians' reading habits. According to the 1998 survey, which, so far as I can tell, was compiled through information that Canadians volunteered, approximately 80 percent of all Canadians from age fifteen on read newspapers, 71 percent read magazines, and 61 percent read books.

Not bad.

Out of the 80 percent who read newspapers, 49 percent read a daily, which means that 39 percent of all Canadians read a daily newspaper.

I'm impressed.

Out of the 71 percent who read a magazine, 57 percent read at least one magazine weekly, which means that 40 percent of all Canadians read at least one magazine a week.

That's great.

And out of the 61 percent of all Canadians who read books, 31 percent read at least a book a week, which means about 19 percent of all Canadians read at least a book a week.

Fifty-two books a year.

Unless, of course, I've done the math wrong. Which is possible.

No doubt this includes students at high schools, colleges, and universities, who are "encouraged" to read. Still, if you look at just the self-confessed readers in the category of twenty-five-year-olds and older, you'll find that the percentage stays exactly the same. Nineteen percent.

So how do they do that? Over four million Canadians reading a book a week, each and every week of the year. Well, some are parents reading to their children. Some are professionals who read for a living. Some are up at the cottage or on a beach somewhere, away from television and the phone.

And the rest?

Well, maybe it's true. Or maybe we Canadians just like to think of ourselves as more literate than we really are.

Not that it matters. What's curious is that there are no statistics for oral literature.

When I raised this question at a scholarly conference once, I was told that the reason we pay attention to written literature is that books are quantifiable, whereas oral literature is not. How can you quantify something that has sound but no physical form, a colleague wanted to

know, something that exists only in the imagination of the
storyteller, cultural ephemera that is always at the whim
of memory, something that needs to be written down to
be . . . whole?

I understand the assumptions: first, that stories, in
order to be complete, must be written down, an easy error
to make, an ethnocentric stumble that imagines all literature in the Americas to have been oral, when in fact,
pictographic systems (petroglyphs, pictographs, and
hieroglyphics) were used by a great many tribes to com-
memorate events and to record stories, while in the valley
of Mexico, the Aztecs maintained a large library of written works that may well have been the rival of the Royal
Library at Alexandria. Written and oral. Side by side.

In the end, though, neither fared any better than the
other. While European diseases and conflicts with explorers and settlers led to the death and displacement of a
great many Native storytellers, superstitious Spanish
priests, keen on saving the Aztecs from themselves,
burned the library at Tenochtitlán to the ground, an event
as devastating as Julius Caesar's destruction of the library
at Alexandria.

In each case, at Tenochtitlán and at Alexandria, stories
were lost. And, in the end, it didn't matter whether these
stories were oral or written.

So much for dependability. So much for permanence.

Though it doesn't take a disaster to destroy a literature. If we stopped telling the stories and reading the
books, we would discover that neglect is as powerful an
agent as war and fire.

In 1980, through a series of mishaps and happenstance, my nine-year-old son and I moved from Salt Lake City, Utah, to Lethbridge, Alberta. The details of the move — divorce, unemployment, depression — are too boring to explicate. The reason for the move, however, was simple. The University of Lethbridge had offered me a job. I had been to Lethbridge before. A good friend of mine, Leroy Little Bear, had brought me up as a speaker for Indian Days at the university. So I had seen the lay of the land. As it were.

And it was flat.

Flat, dry, windy, dusty. Nothing like the Northern California coast that I loved. And the last place on earth I wanted to work. But when you don't have a job, something always looks better than nothing.

So we moved. I bought an old step-side pickup from a government auction, packed everything I owned in the back, strapped my son into the passenger's seat, and headed north.

Just before we got to Sweetgrass and the border between Alberta and Montana, heavy rain turned into heavy hail, and we had to make a run for a freeway overpass. There, under the concrete canopy along with several other cars and trucks, we waited out the storm.

Which wasn't about to give up easily. The hail picked up pace, turning the road in front of us into a skating rink, and my son, who even at nine was not one to put sugar on sorrow, turned to me and said, "Just so we keep it straight, Dad, this was your idea."

The second assumption about written literature is that it has an inherent sophistication that oral literature lacks, that oral literature is a primitive form of written literature, a precursor to written literature, and as we move from the cave to the condo, we slough off the oral and leave it behind.

Like an old skin.

The Kiowa writer N. Scott Momaday, in his novel *House Made of Dawn*, touches on the written and the oral, on the cultural understandings of language and literature. The White man, Momaday argues, takes "such things as words and literatures for granted . . . for nothing in his world is so commonplace. . . . He is sated and insensitive; his regard for language . . . as an instrument of creation has diminished nearly to the point of no return. It may be that he will perish by the Word."

But of his Kiowa grandmother, who could neither read nor write and whose use of language was confined to speech, Momaday says that "her regard for words was always keen in proportion as she depended upon them . . . for her words were medicine; they were magic and invisible. They came from nothing into sound and meaning. They were beyond price; they could neither be bought nor sold. And she never threw words away."[4]

Perhaps it was this quality of medicine and magic that sent nineteenth- and twentieth-century anthropologists and ethnographers west to collect and translate Native stories, thereby "preserving" Native oral literature before it was lost. As a result of these efforts, an impressive body of oral stories is now stored in periodicals and books that one can find at any good research library.

Not that anyone reads them. But they are safe and sound. As it were.

At the same time that social scientists were busy preserving Native oral culture, Native people were beginning to write. Depending on how far you want to stretch the definition of literature, you can begin in the late eighteenth century with Samson Occum, who collected hymns and spirituals, or you can wait until the nineteenth century and begin with George Copway's autobiography or Alice Callahan's novel or E. Pauline Johnson's poetry.

I'm tempted to say the names of all of the early Native writers aloud, though such a long and comprehensive list would probably put everybody to sleep. Still, such a name-dropping exercise might impress you and make me look scholarly and learned.

And truth be told, I can live with that.

Perhaps I could frame such a bibliography as a eulogy to remind myself of where stories come from, a chance to remember that I stand in a circle of storytellers, most of whom will never be published, who have only their imaginations and their voices.

That sounds rather romantic, doesn't it. Circles of storytellers. Oral voices in the night. You can almost hear the violins.

I mean the drums.

The point I wanted to make was that the advent of Native written literature did not, in any way, mark the passing of Native oral literature. In fact, they occupy the same space, the same time. And, if you know where to stand, you can hear the two of them talking to each other.

Robert Alexie's *Porcupines and China Dolls*, for instance, and Harry Robinson's *Write It On Your Heart*, along with Ruby Slipperjack's *Honour the Sun* and Eden Robinson's *Monkey Beach*. A novel, a collection of stories, and two more novels. Canadians all. Though the border doesn't mean that much to the majority of Native people in either country. It is, after all, a figment of someone else's imagination.

But I'll start this discussion of literature with an American example. Partly because I have to, and partly because I have a perverse streak and, at times, would rather annoy than placate.

So, the first thing to say about the advent of the modern period in Native written literature is that it begins with the publication of N. Scott Momaday's 1968 novel *House Made of Dawn*, a book that won the Pulitzer Prize. But what makes the novel special and what allows us to use it as a starting point are the questions that it raises and its concern with narrative strategies. As well as what it avoids.

With the long and problematic history that Native people have had with Europeans in North America, it would be reasonable to expect that, when Native writers took to the novel, they would go to the past for setting in order to argue against the rather lopsided and ethnocentric view of Indians that novelists and historians had created.

James Fenimore Cooper, for instance.

Cooper, whose sympathies lay with the wealthy, landowner class of nineteenth-century America, had a somewhat romantic view of Indians that saw them either as noble or savage. Noble Indians helped Whites and died for their trouble. Savage Indians hindered Whites and died for their trouble. A rather simplistic division. But Cooper took the matter further. What is it, Cooper asked himself, that makes Indians different from Whites? Why is it that Indians and Whites can never come together?

His answer was gifts. Indian gifts. And White gifts.

In *The Deerslayer*, the first (chronologically, that is) of the five Leatherstocking Tales, Cooper's protagonist, Natty Bumppo, a.k.a. Deerslayer, later to be known as Hawkeye, gets into a running philosophical discussion with Henry March, a boorish frontiersman, on the matter of race.

"Now skin makes the man," March tells Deerslayer. "This is reason — else how are people to judge each other? The skin is put on, over all, in order that when a creature or a mortal is fairly seen, you may know at once what to make of him."[5]

Here is the essence of racism. "Skin makes the man." A simple declaration that divides the world up quickly. March believes that anyone who is not White is inferior, but he's a bigot and a scoundrel whose morality is suspect, and readers have little sympathy for the man or his views. Deerslayer, on the other hand, objects to March's simple divisions and offers an explanation for difference that, on the surface, is more complex and balanced.

Indians and Whites, Deerslayer argues, while having different-coloured skin, are still both men, men with "different gifts and traditions, but, in the main, with the same natur'. Both have souls," he tells us, "and both will be held accountable for their deeds in this life."[6]

Though both are not necessarily equal.

"God made us all," Cooper says through Deerslayer, "white, black, red — and no doubt had his own wise intentions in coloring us differently. Still, he made us, in the main, much the same in feelin's, though I'll not deny that he gave each race its gifts. A white man's gifts are Christianized, while a redskin's are more for the wilderness."[7]

As it turns out, March and Deerslayer are not arguing different points of view, they are arguing variations of the same view. Cooper isn't arguing for equality. He's arguing for separation, using some of the same arguments that 1950s America would use for segregating Blacks from Whites. Indians aren't necessarily inferior. They just have different gifts. Their skin colour isn't the problem. It's their natures.

So what exactly are these gifts? What are these natures that mark out a people?

Well, according to Deerslayer, revenge is an Indian gift and forgiveness is a White gift. Indians have devious natures, while Whites believe the best of a person. "You were treacherous, according to your natur'," Deerslayer tells an Indian he has just mortally wounded, "and I was a little oversightful, as I'm apt to be in trusting others."[8]

In the end, all Cooper is doing here is reiterating the basic propagandas that the British would use to justify their subjugation of India, or that the Germans would employ in their extermination of Jews, or that the Jews would utilize to displace Palestinians, or that North Americans would exploit for the internment of the Japanese, or that the U.S. military and the U.S. media would craft into jingoistic slogans in order to make the invasions of other countries — Grenada, Panama, Afghanistan, Iraq — seem reasonable, patriotic, and entertaining to television audiences throughout North America.

Reason and Instinct.

White gifts in Cooper's novel are gifts of Reason. Indian gifts in Cooper's novel are gifts of Instinct.

It would be reasonable to expect Native writers to want to revisit and reconstruct the literary and historical past, but oddly enough — with few exceptions such as James Welch's *Fool's Crow* and *The Heartsong of Charging Elk*, Diane Glancy's *Pushing the Bear*, and Linda Hogan's *Mean Spirit* — contemporary Native writers have shown little interest in using the past as setting, preferring instead to place their fictions in the present.

And I don't have a good answer for why this is true. Though I do have some suspicions. I think that, by the time Native writers began to write in earnest and in numbers, we discovered that the North American version of the past was too well populated, too well defended. By 1968, the cowboy/Indian dichotomy was so firmly in place and had been repeated and re-inscribed so many times that there was no chance of dislodging it from the culture. Like it or not, it was a permanent landmark, and Native writers who went to *that* past ran into the demand that Indians had to be noble and tragic and perform all their duties on horseback.

What Native writers discovered, I believe, was that the North American past, the one that had been created in novels and histories, the one that had been heard on radio and seen on theatre screens and on television, the one that had been part of every school curriculum for the last two hundred years, that past was unusable, for it had not only trapped Native people in a time warp, it also insisted that our past was all we had.

No present.

No future.

And to believe in such a past is to be dead.

Faced with such a proposition and knowing from empirical evidence that we were very much alive, physically and culturally, Native writers began to use the Native present as a way to resurrect a Native past and to imagine a Native future. To create, in words, as it were, a Native universe.

I had been teaching at Lethbridge for about a month when a couple of young men from the Blood reserve arrived at my office. Narcisse Blood and Martin Heavyhead. Both of them played basketball in an all-Native league, and they had come to talk me into playing for the team. I told them I was too old and too slow. I told them I couldn't dribble or shoot or block shots.

It's okay, Narcisse told me, you're nice and big and can get in the way.

So I said yes. I was lonely, wanted to be liked, wanted to be accepted. Even if I couldn't play, I could at least make the effort. But in the first game, I was amazing. Every time I lumbered to the basket, the other players got out of my way. When I took a shot, no one tried to stop me. I scored six points that night. The next game I scored eight.

The matter began to unravel in the third game. One of their guards drove the lane. I stepped in front of him, tried to block the shot, and both of us went down in a heap.

The guard who had run into me leaped up, concerned.

You okay?

Sure, I told him.

Nothing rattled loose, eh?

I have to admit, no one had ever asked me that. Rattled loose?

You know, the guard said, looking embarrassed. The plate.

Plate? I said. What plate?

In your head.

It turned out Narcisse had told the other teams that when I had come up from Salt Lake City, I had run into a hailstorm, lost control of the truck, and flipped it. A serious accident that left me with a plate in my head. Everything was okay as long as I didn't get bumped, because if I did get bumped and the plate slipped, I would go berserk. It happened once during a practice,

Narcisse had told everyone, and the guy was still in the hospital.

I don't have a plate in my head.

And with that imprudent remark, my basketball career went down the toilet. As soon as the rest of the teams in the league found out that they were in no danger from plate slippage, I was a marked man. I don't think I scored two points the rest of the season.

Now, where was I?

Oh, yes. Native writers creating a Native universe. For N. Scott Momaday, the answer, in part, was to write a novel in which aspects of an unfamiliar universe stood close enough to parts of a known world so that the non-Native reader, knowing the one, might recognize the other. Ironically, Christianity, which had been a door barred against Native–non-Native harmony and understanding, suddenly became an open window through which we could see and hear each other.

House Made of Dawn, reduced to a Coles Notes blurb, is the story of a young Native man who returns from World War II to discover that he no longer has a place in the Pueblo world that he left. The return of the Native. No problem here. A common enough theme. Until Momaday begins to complicate it.

The protagonist's name is Abel, a name filled with import for a non-Native audience, conjuring up as it does a whole host of Christian concerns. Abel is Adam and Eve's son and Cain's brother, and it is Abel whom Cain kills.

Which should be the end of the story. But where Abel's story in the Bible ends, Momaday's story begins. And here is Abel's dilemma. When he returns from the horror and destruction of World War II, he discovers that he has no voice — not literally but figuratively — a condition that proves to be symptomatic of a larger confusion, a confusion surrounding the nature of good and evil, not just in the world that Momaday creates but in the world at large as well. In making parts of a Native universe visible, Momaday also examines the assumptions that the White world makes about good and evil. Using the occasion of the war and Abel's trial for killing an albino Indian, Momaday reminds us that within the Christian dichotomy, good and evil always oppose each other.

Which is why war, even with its inherent horror and destruction, can be presented and pursued as a righteous activity. And it's why Abel's trial is not concerned with the reasons he killed the albino but only with the simpler matter of whether or not he was responsible for the man's death. These questions, good/bad, guilty/innocent, are simple questions, their answers familiar and satisfying for Momaday's non-Native audience, and these moments of recognition allow him to re-ask the same questions, this time within a Pueblo context.

And here, the answers are not so familiar, not so easy, for within the Pueblo world, evil and good are not so much distinct and opposing entities as they are tributaries of the same river. In this world, old men in white leggings chase evil in the night, "not in the hope of anything, but hopelessly; neither in fear nor hatred nor despair of evil, but simply in recognition and with respect."[9] And strong men on strong horses try to pull a live rooster out of the sand, only to destroy the bird by beating it to pieces against a fellow rider.

The runners after evil and the feast of Santiago. Strange moments in a strange world.

But not good and evil.

Rather, two ceremonies, ceremonies that describe a part of the complexity of the lives of the Pueblo people, ceremonies where the basic Christian oppositions have little meaning. For both of these moments are celebrations, acknowledgements, if you will, one of the presence of evil in the world while doing nothing to encourage or prevent it, the other of the need for sacrifice and renewal.

The temptation here, of course, is to dissect each scene, separate out the elements, and organize them according to colour. The ceremonial run is good. The presence of evil is bad. The rooster pull is a form of competition and therefore good. The destruction of the rooster by beating it to death against another human being is cruel.

How we love our binaries.

But what Momaday and other Native writers suggest is that there are other ways of imagining the world, ways that do not depend so much on oppositions as they do on co-operations, and they raise the tantalizing question of what else one might do if confronted with the appearance of evil.

So just how would we manage a universe in which the attempt to destroy evil is seen as a form of insanity?

Relax. It's only fiction.

Besides, Native writers aren't arguing that evil isn't evil or that it doesn't exist. They're suggesting that trying to destroy it is misguided, even foolish. That the attempt risks disaster.

But you don't need Native writers to tell you that.

Grab a copy of *Moby Dick* and consider the saga of Captain Ahab, wrapped in rage, as he roams the oceans in search of the great white whale, accomplishing little more than the destruction of his ship and crew; or turn on your television and watch a vengeful United States, burdened with the arms of war, bomb the world into goodness and supply-side capitalism, destroying American honour and credibility in the process.

Of course, Native writers are engaged in much more than a literary debate over the nature of good and evil. While writers such as N. Scott Momaday and Leslie Silko examine these tensions, other Native writers have taken on other concerns. Gerald Vizenor borrows traditional figures, such as the Trickster, re-imagines them within a contemporary context, and sets them loose in a sometimes modern, sometimes post-apocalyptic world. James Welch looks at the question of identity, of place, and the value of names. Louise Erdrich explores the shadow land of resistance. Simon Ortiz captures the rhythms of traditional song and ceremony in his poetry. Tomson Highway handles the difficult matter of reserve community and gender and family relationships. Lee Maracle and Jeannette Armstrong show how traditional wisdom and customs can suggest ways to conduct oneself in the present.

But what is most satisfying is knowing that there are Native writers whose names I have never heard of, who are, at this minute, creating small panoramas of contemporary Native life by looking backward and forward with the same glance.

Not so differently from non-Native writers.

The magic of Native literature — as with other literatures — is not in the themes of the stories — identity, isolation, loss, ceremony, community, maturation, home — it is in the way meaning is refracted by cosmology, the way understanding is shaped by cultural paradigms.

Narcisse Blood is a good friend. One time he took me out to visit his grandfather, who lived in a small house on the reserve. The old man had a garden, and he took me through it, showing me each plant. Later we had tea in his kitchen.

Did I know about the big storm? he asked.

I had to admit that I didn't.

It was a big one, he said. It came up quick and hard.

So I told him about my trip from Salt Lake City to Lethbridge and how we had been trapped under a freeway overpass by a storm.

Yes, those storms can be tricky, he told me. You see those tomatoes out there?

From the kitchen window you could see his garden. The tomato plants were just beginning to produce fruit.

When that storm came through, I was just getting ready to pick my tomatoes. They were big and red. Real ripe. But that storm beat me to it. First the rain. And then the hail.

And here the old man stopped and helped himself to more tea. And then he sat back and looked at the table.

I tried to be sympathetic. You must have been upset, I said.

Nope, said the old man, without even the hint of a smile. Always good to have some ketchup.

During the 1960s, when many of us hoped that love would prove more powerful than hate, herds of young people — "hippies," if you were from Yorkville, or "flower children," if you were from Haight-Ashbury, or "bums," if you were from Pittsburgh — made their way to reserves and reservations throughout North America, sure that Native people possessed the secret to life. Or at least something middle-class North America didn't have.

That something turned out to be poverty. Or at least poverty was what they saw. And as quickly as they arrived, most left. After all, living simply was one thing, being poor was quite another.

What was not readily apparent at first glance from the window of a Volkswagen van or from the comfort of a refitted school bus was the intimate relationship that Native people had with the land. And here I am not talking about the romantic and spiritual clichés that have become so popular with advertisers, land developers, and well-meaning people with backpacks. While the relationship that Native people have with the land certainly has a spiritual aspect to it, it is also a practical matter that balances respect with survival. It is an ethic that can be seen in the decisions and actions of a community and that is contained in the songs that Native people sing and the stories that they tell about the nature of the world and their place in it, about the webs of responsibilities that bind all things. Or, as the Mohawk writer Beth Brant put it, "We do not worship nature. We are part of it."[10]

This is the territory of Native oral literature. And it is the territory of contemporary Native written literature. The difference is this: instead of waiting for you to come to us, as we have in the past, written literature has allowed us to come to you.

I'd like to say that both efforts have been worth it. But I'm not sure they have. It seems to me that sharing our oral stories with ethnographers and anthropologists and sharing our written stories with non-Native audiences have produced pretty much the same results. And, at best, they have been mixed.

Some of the essential questions that Native story-tellers and writers have raised about, say, the nature of good and evil have been ignored. The Trickster figure — a complex arrangement of appetites and desires — has been reduced to cartoon elements. The land as a living entity has become a mantra for industries that destroy the environment. Mother earth, a potent phrase for Native people, has been abused to the point where it has no more power or import than the word "freedom" tumbling out of George W. Bush's mouth.

It is true that scholars have taken on the task of considering Native literatures within a postcolonial context and this, in and of itself, has been heartening, but most of us don't live in the university, and I can only imagine that the majority of Native people would be more amused by the gymnastics of theoretical language — hegemony and subalternity, indeed — than impressed.

All of which will sound as if I'm suggesting that Native writers should only write for Native readers, that these are our stories, that we should tell them for ourselves.

If only things were that simple.

Yet, truth be told, this is what it appears we are beginning to do. Remember those four writers I started to mention? The Canadians (if you believe in maps): Robert Alexie and Harry Robinson, Ruby Slipperjack and Eden Robinson? These four are creating their fictions, I believe, primarily for a Native audience, making a conscious decision not so much to ignore non-Native readers as to write for the very people they write about.

No, I can't prove it.

So it's lucky for me that literary analysis is not about proof, only persuasion. In our cynical world, where suspicion is a necessity, insisting that something is true is not nearly as powerful as suggesting that something might be true.

So allow me to *suggest* that we look at Robert Alexie's novel *Porcupines and China Dolls*. Just as an example. One of the more intriguing offerings in 2002, the book neither generated much critical acclaim nor made any of the shortlists for literary prizes. The blurb on the jacket of the Stoddart edition warns us that this is the "story of a journey from the dark side of reality . . . a story of pain and healing, of making amends and finding truth, of the inability of a people to hold on to their way of life."

Certainly sounds like the Indians we know.

The jacket copy also makes it sound as though *Porcupines and China Dolls* could be one of those depressing indictments of social policy and racial bias, a case study docudrama with all the romantic underpinnings and tragic disasters of a good soap opera. But Alexie is not writing *that* story, and he is not writing for *that* audience.

"In order to understand this story," Alexie says in the first chapter, "it is important to know the People and where they came from and what they went through,"[11] and for the first two chapters, Alexie gives the reader a lightning-quick tour that includes a mention of creation, the arrival of Whites in 1789, the arrival of missionaries in 1850, and a brief history of life at a residential school.

All in the first sixteen pages.

For the non-Native reader, this briefing is too little to do much good. For the Native reader (and in this case, a particular Native reader) who knows the history and the way the weight of this knowing settles over the rest of the book, it is simply a way of saying "once upon a time."

In *Porcupines and China Dolls*, James Nathan and Jake Noland return from Aberdeen residential school, where the girls had been scrubbed and powdered to look like china dolls and the boys had been scrubbed and sheared to look like porcupines, and where each night, when the children cried in their beds, the sound was like "a million porcupines crying in the dark."[12]

Native writers are particularly keen on the return of the Native. Momaday's Abel returns from World War II, as does Silko's Tayo. James Welch's unnamed narrator in

Winter in the Blood returns from the city, as do June and Albertine in Louise Erdrich's *Love Medicine*. In *Slash*, Jeannette Armstrong's Tommy Kelasket comes home from jail, as does Garnet Raven in Richard Wagamese's *Keeper'n Me*. And, for that matter, in my first novel, *Medicine River*, Will also comes home.

These returns often precipitate a quest or a discovery or a journey. For James and Jake, their return involves simply a sorting out, an ordering of relationships, memories, and possibilities, an attempt to come to terms with the past, an attempt to find a future.

I suspect that many people who come to this book will leave it annoyed and/or puzzled and/or bored by the novel's biting satire, by its refusal to resolve the tensions that it creates, and by a narrative style that privileges repetition, hyperbole, and orality as storytelling strategies. Non-Native readers will probably tire of hearing about the sound of "a million porcupines crying in the dark," and cringe at the mantra of people growing ten, then twenty, then thirty, then forty feet tall with pride as they "disclose" the sexual abuse they suffered at residential school or the relentless cycle of attempts and failures as characters try to put their lives in order. But in all this, there is a delightful inventiveness of tone, a strength of purpose that avoids the hazards of the lament and allows the characters the pleasure of laughing at themselves and their perils. For the Native reader, these continuing attempts of the community to right itself and the omnipresent choruses of sadness and humour, of tragedy and sarcasm, become, in the end, an honour song of sorts, a song many of us have heard before.

All Natives?

Of course not.

There's no magic in the blood that provides us with an ethnic memory. But there are more of us who know this song than there should be.

So what? What difference does it make if we write for a non-Native audience or a Native audience, when the fact of the matter is that we need to reach both?

Take Louis Owens, for instance. Maybe if *Porcupines and China Dolls* had been written earlier and more people had read the novel and understood the story, Louis and the rest of those workers wouldn't have had to walk home that summer.

I don't believe it, but then, I'm a cynic.

Maybe if Louis had had the chance to read Alexie's book, he would have gotten on that plane and gone to the conference.

I'm not sure I believe this, either.

Ironically, in many ways, Louis's story is Alexie's story. At the beginning and the end of *Porcupines and China Dolls*, James puts the barrel of a gun in his mouth and pulls the trigger. And in the novel, as in life, whether he lives or dies depends on which story he believes.

And this I do believe.

Which is why I tell those three stories over and over again. The story of the time my son and I came to Canada. The story of my short career as a basketball player. The story of an old man and his garden.

And there are others.

I tell them to myself, to my friends, sometimes to

strangers. Because they make me laugh. Because they are a particular kind of story. Saving stories, if you will. Stories that help keep me alive.

Of course, you don't have to pay attention to any of these stories. Louis's story is not particularly cheery. Alexie's story doesn't have a demonstrably happy ending. Neither participates fully in Western epistemologies, and my three don't have a moral centre nor are they particularly illuminating.

But help yourself to one if you like.

Take Louis's story, for instance. It's yours. Do with it what you will. Cry over it. Get angry. Forget it. But don't say in the years to come that you would have lived your life differently if only you had heard this story.

You've heard it now.

V

WHAT IS IT ABOUT US
THAT YOU DON'T LIKE?

THERE IS A STORY I KNOW. It's about the earth and how it floats in space on the back of a turtle. I've heard this story many times, and each time someone tells the story, it changes. Sometimes the change is simply in the voice of the storyteller. Sometimes the change is in the details. Sometimes in the order of events. Other times it's the dialogue or the response of the audience. But in all the tellings of all the tellers, the world never leaves the turtle's back. And the turtle never swims away.

One time, it was in Moncton I think, a woman with a baby in the audience asked about the turtle and the earth. If the earth was on the back of a turtle, what was below the turtle? Another turtle, the storyteller told her. And below that turtle? Another turtle. And below that? Another turtle.

The woman began to chuckle and rock her baby, enjoying the game, I imagine. So how many turtles are there? she wanted to know. The storyteller shrugged. No one knows for sure, he told her, but it's turtles all the way down.

The truth about stories is that that's all we are.

"There are stories that take seven days to tell," says the Cherokee storyteller Diane Glancy. "There are other stories that take you all your life."[1]

I like Coyote stories. And one of my favourites is the one about Coyote and the Ducks. Not the one where the Ducks dance around with their eyes shut while Coyote grabs them one by one and tosses them in his hunting bag. And not the one where he tries to talk the Ducks into teaching him how to fly.

The other one.

The one about the feathers.

And it goes like this.

In the days when everything was beginning, and animals were still talking to humans, Coyote had a beautiful fur coat of which he was very vain. Every day Coyote would come down to the river and look at his reflection.

Goodness, but I have a lovely coat, Coyote would whisper to the water, and then he would give himself a hug.

One day while he was admiring his fur coat, he saw six Ducks singing and dancing and swimming around in circles. Back and forth they went, spinning and turning and diving and leaping in the sunshine. Now, in those days, Ducks had lovely long feathers that shimmered and flashed like the Northern Lights. And when the Ducks had finished singing and dancing and swimming around in circles, they carefully cleaned each feather and straightened it and fluffed it up, so that it glowed even more than before.

That is certainly a wonderful song, said Coyote, who was a little dizzy from watching the Ducks swim around in circles. And that is certainly a beautiful dance.

Yes, said the Ducks. We sing to keep everything in balance, and we dance for peace and generosity, and we swim around in circles to remind everyone of our relationship to the earth.

And those are certainly lovely feathers, said Coyote.

Yes, said those Ducks, they certainly are.

I would certainly like to have one of those lovely feathers, said Coyote. It would go so well with my excellent fur coat.

Now, in those days, Ducks were very agreeable. All right, they said. Just be careful with it, for we are quite fond of our feathers.

I will, said Coyote, and he stuck the feather behind his left ear and ran off to show it to all his friends.

What do you think of my feather? he asked everyone he saw.

It certainly is unusual, said Bear, who tended to be more critical than he needed to be. Too bad you only have one, for now you look a little lopsided.

Oh, dear, said Coyote, and he ran back to the river to find the Dancing Ducks.

Excuse me, Coyote shouted, would it be possible to get another feather?

Another feather? said the Ducks.

Yes, said Coyote, as you can see, having only one feather makes me appear lopsided.

Ah, said the Ducks. You're right. You do look a little lopsided. And the Ducks gave Coyote another feather. But this is the last one, they said. Don't ask for any more, for we need our feathers.

I won't, said Coyote. I promise.

And Coyote stuck the feather behind his right ear and ran off to show it to all his friends.

Aren't these the most beautiful feathers you've ever seen? said Coyote.

They certainly are, said Raven. And such an improvement on that ratty fur coat.

You don't like my wonderful fur coat? said Coyote.

Fur's okay, said Raven, but feathers are so much better.

They are? said Coyote.

Certainly, said Raven, stretching out one wing as far as she could. Anyone who is anyone has feathers.

Well, you can imagine poor Coyote's distress. If Raven was right, and she was seldom wrong, then fur had somehow fallen out of fashion. Oh dear, oh dear, said Coyote, I'm going to need more feathers. And back to the river he went.

When the Ducks saw Coyote waiting for them on the bank, they ruffled their feathers and looked quite annoyed.

We hope you haven't come to ask us for more feathers, said the Ducks.

I wouldn't do that, said Coyote, and he smiled so all his teeth showed. I've come to protect you.

Protect us? said the Ducks. From what?

Human Beings, said Coyote, who on occasion can be clever. I heard them talking. They plan to steal all your feathers.

Steal our feathers! shouted the Ducks.

They might even try to eat you, said Coyote.

Eat us! said the Ducks. Human Beings eat Ducks?

Coyote pretended to shudder. You'd be amazed what they will eat, he said.

But then who will sing for them? said the Ducks. Who will dance for them? Who will remind them of their relationship with the earth?

Never mind that stuff, said Coyote, and he lowered his eyes and lowered his voice and looked around to make sure no one was watching. I have a plan that might save you. You give me half of your feathers and I'll pretend to be a Duck and I'll let the Human Beings chase me around until they get tired and give up.

Half our feathers? said the Ducks.

You'll get to keep the other half, said Coyote. And you'll be safe.

So the Ducks talked it over, and they agreed that half their feathers was better than no feathers, and certainly better than being eaten.

But what happens if they catch you? said the Ducks.

Oh, don't worry, said Coyote, they won't catch me. For I am exceptionally fast and very tricky.

Well, you can imagine just how good Coyote looked with his long shimmering Duck feathers. Even Bear was impressed.

They're okay, said Bear. If you like that sort of thing.

Look at me, Coyote cried, as he ran through the woods and over the mountains and down into the valleys, the feathers trailing behind him, flashing in the light. Look at me!

But Coyote was not very careful with the feathers. He didn't clean them or straighten them or fluff them up as the Ducks had done, and, after a few weeks, the feathers were bent and dirty and ragged, and they looked very, very sad, for they no longer shimmered and glowed.

We can't have this, said Coyote, and he threw the feathers away and went back to the river.

When the Ducks saw Coyote without the feathers they had given him, they were concerned.

What happened to all our feathers? said the Ducks.

The Human Beings took them, said Coyote. They caught me while I was sleeping.

How horrible, said the Ducks.

What's worse, said Coyote, is I need more feathers.

More feathers! shrieked the Ducks. Absolutely not! No, no, no, no!

Then, said Coyote, puffing out his chest as best he could, we'll fight them together.

Fight? Fight whom? said the Ducks, who were well versed in the rules of grammar.

Human Beings, of course, said Coyote. For they can be very fierce when they don't get what they want.

Well, the Ducks didn't know what to do. They talked about flying away but their long feathers made flying tiring, and they talked about swimming away but they didn't know where they would go, and they talked about running away but their legs were too short to do that. Besides, they were happy just where they were.

These Human Beings, said the Ducks, what is it about us that they don't like?

Oh, they like you well enough, said Coyote. They just like your feathers better.

Now, I could finish this story but you already know what's going to happen, don't you? The Ducks are going to keep giving up their beautiful long feathers. Coyote is going to make a mess of things. The world is going to change. And no one is going to be particularly happy.

Besides, this particular story is a long one that takes days to tell. A good storyteller can keep it going for a week. We don't really have the time. And there are other stories that are just as much fun and much shorter.

Such as the one we like to tell ourselves about injustices and atrocities and how most of them have happened in the past. We tell ourselves that, as we have progressed as a species, we have gotten smarter and more compassionate. We say of slavery, for example, yes, that was a horror. We know better now, and we won't make that mistake again. Of course, segregation was a problem, too, wasn't it.

And if we do make such a mistake in our lifetime, say, for instance, dumping raw sewage into the ocean or dropping bombs on people, we say that this was an aberration, a creature of the moment. We say that it was the times, that the fault was in our stars, that you had to have been there. As if what we did was set in motion by natural forces outside our control, something that caught us unawares or took us by surprise.

Indians, for example.

One of the surprising things about Indians is that we're still here. After some five hundred years of vigorous encouragement to assimilate and disappear, we're still here.

Don't worry, this is not the prelude to a flock of sweeping generalizations and caustic complaints. I'm not going to carry on about genocide or residential schools or blankets infected with smallpox (no one has ever been able to prove that one anyway). I'm not going to mention Big Bear or Louis Riel or the Lubicon Lake Cree or the Mi'kmaq at Burnt Church or the Innu at Davis Inlet or Dudley George at Ipperwash or Neil Stonechild and the Saskatoon police.

I'm not going to talk about the forced removal of Indians from their homes or the reserve system or the paternalistic manner in which governments manage the affairs of Native people.

What I want to talk about is legislation.

In the old days, when we were still a problem, the military solution was as good as any. But after a hundred years or so of killing each other, both sides decided that wars were expensive. They cost money. They cost lives. And so, in North America, where Indians and the British and the French and the Americans spent a good deal of time and effort fighting each other, it was eventually agreed that making treaties was better than making war. A rather enlightened decision, if I do say so. The problem was that, like the Ducks in the Coyote story, the first rule of treaties was that Indians had to give up most of their feathers in order to keep some of their feathers for themselves.

At the time, treaties were a poor deal for Indians and a good deal for Whites. But lately, they've been a better deal for Indians and not such a good deal for Whites, because like Coyote, Whites haven't been happy with only most of the feathers.

You might suppose that in the story about Coyote and the Ducks, eventually, Coyote winds up with all the Ducks' feathers, and, in fact, that is what happens.

Sort of.

While the Ducks do give up all their large feathers, the new feathers that grow in are much smaller, and they don't shimmer quite so much and they don't glow quite as brightly as before, and Coyote leaves the Ducks alone for the moment as he looks around for more valuable acquisitions.

With Native people, while our land base was drastically reduced in the early years of treaty making, that erosion has slowed. Even stopped in some areas. Mind you, we don't have much land left, but feathers are feathers. And even if all the large ones are gone, after a while, Coyote is going to come back, looking for the smaller ones. For he has an insatiable appetite.

However, there is a problem with this story: as long as there are Indians, there will be a plethora of "Indian things." Feathers, if you will. Indian land. Indian rights. Indian resources. Indian claims.

Gnarly, difficult, tempting things that try the patience of governments, affront corporations, annoy the general public, and frighten the horses.

What to do?

What to do?

Indians. You can't live with them. You can't shoot them.

Well, not anymore.

So it's just as well we have legislation.

And legislation, in relation to Native people, has had two basic goals. One, to relieve us of our land, and two, to legalize us out of existence. I know that probably sounds like a rather harsh and cynical statement, and it's not completely true. In the Proclamation of 1763, for example, the British government, partly out of fear of the French presence in North America, allowed that each tribe was an independent nation subject only to tribal law and exempt from British law. But this was a mistake that, later, American and Canadian governments would not repeat.

In 1887, the U.S. Congress passed the General Allotment Act, or the Dawes Act as it was popularly known. Driven by the government's desire to control tribes, by the desire of settlers for cheap land, and by the popular notion that land set aside for Indians was the antithesis of North American values and fair play, the General Allotment Act sought to "re-imagine" tribes and tribal land.

Assisting in this matter was a group of reformers, known euphemistically as "Friends of the Indian," who felt that breaking up the tribal estate and turning Native people into landowners would help rescue them from their communal but primitive state and hurry them into the mainstream as full and functioning members of society. The key to this, as far as the Friends were concerned, was private ownership of land and an appreciation for the concept of profit.

Merrill E. Gates, one of the Friends, summed it up in a speech on Indian reform. "We have, to begin with," said Gates, "the absolute need of awakening in the savage Indian broader desires and ampler wants. To bring him out of savagery into citizenship we must make the Indian more intelligently selfish before we can make him unselfishly intelligent. We need to awaken in him wants. In his dull savagery he must be touched by the wings of the divine angel of discontent. The desire for property of his own may become an intense educating force. The wish for a home of his own awakens him to new efforts. Discontent with the teepee and the starving rations of the Indian camp in winter is needed to get the Indian out of the blanket and into trousers — and trousers with pockets in them, and with a pocket that aches to be filled with dollars."[2]

And the Ducks thought they had problems.

The heart of the act lay in the division of each reservation into pieces. Indians got some of the pieces — as a rule, 160 acres went to each head of household — while the surplus was auctioned off or sold to White settlers. Indians would become citizens, and magic, presto, be transformed into . . . well, not Indians.

Of course, this isn't exactly what happened, but while the act was in effect — from 1887 to 1934 — the legislation was able to reduce the tribal estate in the United States from 150 million acres to about 48 million acres. Native people would have probably lost more land but the act was repealed in 1934 and besides, by then, much of the land that was left was desert.

Canada, which is generally seen as lagging behind the United States in most things — capitalism, taxation, aggression — actually took the lead in legislating Indians out of existence with the 1876 Indian Act.

It would be too torturous a journey to try to explicate the Indian Act at one sitting, for it is a magical piece of legislation that twists and slides through time, transforming itself and the lives of Native people at every turn. And sprinkled throughout the act, which, among other things, paternalistically defines who is an Indian and who is not, are amendments that can make Indians disappear in a twinkle.

An 1880 amendment allowed for the automatic enfranchisement of any Indian who obtained a university degree.

Get a degree and, poof, you're no longer an Indian.

Serve in the military and, abracadabra, you're no longer an Indian.

Become a clergyman or a lawyer and, presto, no more Indian.

Legislative magic.

Duncan Campbell Scott, the deputy superintendent general of Indian affairs (among other things), speaking candidly in 1920 of Canadian Indian policy said, "Our object is to continue until there is not a single Indian in Canada that has not been absorbed into the body politic and there is no Indian question, and no Indian department."[3]

Hocus-pocus!

Indians. Now you see them. Now you don't.

If you're a scholar of Native history, you're probably waiting for me to get to the U.S. Indian Reorganization Act of 1934. Sometimes called the "Indian Magna Carta" (though I have no idea why), it marked a departure from the general run of legislation that sought to appropriate the Indian estate and to assimilate Indians.

In particular, the act guaranteed to Indians the right to practise traditional religions. It ended the General Allotment Act and allowed that any remaining surplus lands from that process should be returned to the appropriate tribes. It re-established tribal governments. It promoted bilingual education. It even provided the secretary of the interior with an annual appropriation of some two million dollars to buy back portions of Indian land that had been lost, and, from 1934 to 1947, the Native land base in the United States was actually increased by almost four million acres.

So why do I sound unhappy?

After all, the Indian Reorganization Act was a step in a different direction than North American legislation had been taking. Or, more properly, it was a stumble. For in spite of making its way through Congress and in spite of having many of its ideas implemented, the Indian Reorganization Act went against the national temper.

That's a polite way of saying that it annoyed too many people to be successful or long lived. Politicians were opposed to it because it inhibited their free run at Indian land. The clergy, wanting to maintain their religious monopolies, were appalled that Indians could now choose between their traditional beliefs and Christianity. Bureaucrats, afraid that the basic premise of the act suggested that they had not done the job of advocating Indian interests, complained that the new rules and regulations were difficult to administer and impossible to enforce. Even Indians argued against it. After all, in every other instance when the government had come along with a program that was going to make their lives better, things usually got worse.

In 1964, I caught a tramp steamer out of San Francisco and worked my way to New Zealand. I don't know exactly why I went. Adventure, I suppose. That must have been it.

New Zealand was a beautiful country, but it had a problem. Deer. Some bright lad had decided to import deer so erstwhile hunters would have something bigger to shoot than possums and trout, and because the deer had no natural enemies — other than the aforementioned hunters — they multiplied and began eating up the countryside. This caused a great deal of erosion in forests and a great deal of consternation in the forest industry, and the government, in response to complaints from their lumber constituents, put together a band of merry men to roam the woods and control the problem.

Deer cullers.

I needed a job, and deer culling, for reasons I can no longer remember, sounded exciting, and before the week was out, I found myself heading into the woods with the sun above me, a knapsack on my back, a rifle slung over my shoulder, a song in my heart.

Follow the stream, the government man had told me when he dropped me off at the trailhead. Eight miles in, start looking for the cabin.

Anyone who has ever gone hiking knows that eight miles along a stream in the woods is not the same as eight miles walking a paved road. By the time the sun disappeared, I wasn't sure I was any closer to the cabin than I had been when I started.

Indian lost in the woods.

It's a little embarrassing to admit this. But there I was. Lost. In the wilds of New Zealand, tripping over supplejack, wading through cold water, wondering if this was how the country got rid of tourists on thirty-day visas who tried to work illegally.

I was about to give up and find a cold spot to spend the night when I heard a voice and saw a light coming through the trees.

Hey! the voice said, over the clatter of the water. You the Indian?

The Indian Reorganization Act had a thirteen-year lifespan. Some scholars argue that World War II cut it short, and this could be true because by the time Americans came home from Europe and the dust of conflict and nuclear bombs had settled, the Indian Reorganization Act was replaced by another piece of legislation that did not share the IRA's concern for the cultural, social, or political life of Native people.

In 1953 the U.S. Congress passed House Concurrent Resolution 108, more commonly known as the Termination Act. If anyone thought that the Indian Reorganization Act was a shift in the winds of racism, then they would have been surprised to see termination blow in from the west. But for those who knew that the IRA was just a lull in the storm, termination came as no surprise.

The goal of House Concurrent Resolution 108 was to abolish Indians. It sought to accomplish this by terminating federal treaty obligations and special concessions to all tribes, dismantling reservations and "liberating" Native people from poverty and exclusion, and moving them to more urban centres where assimilation would be quick and painless.

This effort was managed by the commissioner of Indian affairs, Dillon S. Myer, who, ironically, had been the director of the War Relocation Authority, which had imprisoned over one hundred thousand Japanese Americans during World War II, and by Arthur Watkins, a senator from Utah whose dislike for Indians was legendary, as was his insatiable appetite for Indian land and resources. Between 1954 and 1962, Congress stripped sixty-one tribes of all federal services and protection.

Coyotes and Ducks.

Canada followed suit sixteen years later with its own termination plan, the 1969 White Paper. Brought in under the Trudeau government with the able assistance of then minister of Indian affairs Jean Chrétien, the 1969 White Paper, even though it never became official government policy, was virtually a carbon copy of House Concurrent Resolution 108. Both had a single goal. To get government out of the "Indian business."

Or, conversely, to get Indians out of the government's business.

They were sorry. Governments, that is. Sorry that they had promised Indians anything. Sorry that they had made treaties with Native people. Sorry that they had given First Nations the impression that they had any special rights under Canadian or international law.

Sorry, sorry, sorry.

And while they were apologizing and complaining, governments were also convincing themselves that they had given these things to Native people out of the goodness of their hearts, that Native rights were something that had flowed from governmental largesse, or, to restate the matter in the dubious phrasing of philanthropic neologisms, that Native rights had been "gifted" to Native people.

It's a lovely sentiment, isn't it. Gifts. The Great White Mother and Father and their Red Children sitting around a Christmas tree, enjoying the holidays, the Indians eager to see what presents their parents have bought for them.

A Currier and Ives moment.

And if you point out that all of these so-called gifts were paid for by Native people, sometimes more than once, and that treaties are legal, binding documents that cannot be dispensed with just because one party suddenly finds them inconvenient, bureaucrats, politicians, and an uninformed public roll their collective eyes and mumble platitudes about the "need to move ahead" or the danger of "living in the past" or the fact that "times change."

Deer cullers worked in pairs. Two men in a small log cabin with a fireplace. No amenities unless you wanted to count silence. The guy who found me in the river trying to look, well, not lost was an ex-Australian named Paul Gibson and he was, by and large, an interesting guy. Most cullers saw the job as a temporary thing. Paul saw it as a career. Living simply in the woods, living off the land, culling deer until all the deer in the country had been culled.

There are things that have value, Paul told me that first night as we drank tea in the cabin, and there are things that don't, and the trick to happiness is knowing which one you are. Deer and sheep both eat the vegetation and can cause erosion that will ruin the forest industry, but sheep have value and deer don't, so that's why we shoot them.

It was an intriguing philosophy, one with a certain amount of merit.

Take me, for instance, he said. I don't have no value. That's why I stay here and hunt the deer. What about you?

I told him I thought I had some value.

No sense kidding yourself, he said. Guy like you runs away and comes to New Zealand to live in the woods with a guy like me and hunt deer. You see what I mean?

I told him I wasn't planning on staying forever, that I just needed some money to get started.

Indians, he said. They're pretty much like Maoris, aren't they?

More or less, I told him.

Then you and the deer should get along just fine.

Okay. Let's forget about the past for a moment.

After all, everything I've mentioned so far is at least thirty years old, most of it over a hundred. So let's look at the present, and, in particular, at the U.S. Indian Arts and Crafts Act and the Canadian Bill c-31.

Both are "termination" legislation (if you're American) or "enfranchisement" legislation (if you're Canadian), and unlike earlier legislation that implicitly asked the question "Who is an Indian?" these newer offerings ask the more modern question, "Whom will we allow to be an Indian?"

In the United States, the Indian Arts and Crafts Act was enacted to keep cheap reproductions of Native arts and crafts off the market and to ensure that, if something said "Made by an Indian," it was. Within the legislation were fines for fraudulent representation, but, more importantly, there were also rules and regulations that described who could be an Indian and who could not.

According to the act, an Indian tribe is any tribe, band, nation, Alaskan Native village, or other organized group or community that is recognized as eligible for the special programs and services provided by the United States to Indians because of their status as Indians, or any Indian group that has been formally recognized as an Indian tribe by a state legislature or a state commission or similar organization legislatively vested with state tribal recognition authority.

The term "Indian" means any individual who is a member of an Indian tribe or, for the purposes of the act, is certified as an Indian artisan by an Indian tribe.

It's a well-meaning law that was aimed at unscrupulous businesses and individuals selling arts and crafts as "Indian made" when in fact they were not, and it allows members of the public to feel secure in their purchases. And the act has hefty punishments for violations. Individuals who violate the law can be fined up to $250,000 and sent to prison for five years, or both. Businesses that violate the act can face civil penalties and fines up to $1 million.

The only problem is that there are Indian tribes that are not federally or state recognized, and there are individual Indians who, for one reason or another, aren't federally recognized and don't have tribal status.

Shadow Indians.

Grey Indians.

Not really Indians at all.

And if these Shadow Indians produce any arts and crafts for sale, they may not refer to themselves as "Indian artists" or by a tribal designation. No matter what their ancestry, community, or background. Just how big is this problem? How many Shadow Indians does this law affect? Does the value of the law outweigh the problems it might cause for a few individuals?

Well, those really aren't the questions, are they?

In the case of Canada's Bill c-31, you have a similar but different conundrum. In 1985, Bill c-31 amended the Indian Act, in part to redress the discrimination against Native women. Prior to c-31 any Indian woman who married a non-Indian or a non-status Indian automatically lost her status, as did any children. The same was not true for Indian men. If they married a non-Indian or a non-status Indian, the woman gained status, as did her children.

Bill c-31 allowed Native women who had lost status because of the Indian Act to regain status, along with their children. And in that respect, the bill was a great success.

Since the act was amended in 1985, some hundred thousand Native people who were non-status because of the discriminatory provisions of the Indian Act have been able to regain their status. And if we look at that figure alone, it would appear that Bill c-31 is about the business of creating new Indians (as it were) rather than legislating us out of existence.

So before Bill c-31, you could gain status or lose status through marriage depending on gender. After Bill c-31, no one could gain or lose status through marriage. You would suppose then that status is safe, protected by legislation, approved by the government, available to every treaty Indian in Canada.

Did I mention about appearances being deceiving? Status, as it is currently defined, is safe only as long as status Indians marry status Indians and their children marry status Indians. The minute a status Indian marries out of status, their children and their children's children are at risk.

Because, as it turns out, while you can't gain or lose status through marriage, your children can.

And here's how it works.

A status Indian marries a status Indian. They have two children, both of whom are status. One child marries a status person and the other child marries a non-status person. The children produced by the status/status couple are status. The children produced by the status/non-status couple are status.

Nothing amiss so far.

Now those children get married. The child from the status/status couple marries a status person and the child from the status/non-status couple marries another non-status person. The children from the status/status/status couple are status. The children from the status/non-status/non-status couple are not. Even if everyone married full-blood Indians. Even though everyone has status great-grandparents.

It's actually more fun than I'm making it, because within the category of status are two subcategories called, euphoniously enough, six-ones and six-twos, referring, of course, to the sections of the legislation that create status. Six-one Indians are status and, for legal purposes, are considered to be full-bloods even if they aren't, while six-two Indians are status and for legal purposes considered to be half-bloods even if they aren't.

Now I won't swear that this is absolutely accurate, but as I understand it the effects of the Indian Act and Bill C-31 are as follows: Six-ones who marry six-ones produce six-one children. Six-ones who marry six-twos produce six-one children. Six-ones who marry non-status produce six-two children.

And six-twos who marry six-twos, or who marry non-status, produce non-status children. And those children can never, ever be status.

Now that's a good trick.

But what the hell happened?

If we were in the States, the answer would be blood quantum. But here in Canada we have what is called the "two-generation cut-off clause." Marry out of status for two generations, and the children from the last union are non-status.

Oh, you can continue to call yourself an Indian, but you can't live on a reserve. You can continue to tell people that you're Cree or Blackfoot or Ojibway or Mohawk, but you can't vote in band elections. You can go to powwows, sing at a drum, sell arts and crafts if you like, but you are no longer eligible for treaty benefits, and neither are your children or their children or their children right down to the end of time.

The two-generation cut-off clause.

No need to send in the cavalry with guns blazing. Legislation will do just as nicely.

And right now about 50 percent of status Indians are

marrying non-status folk. No one knows for sure how long it will take, but according to John Borrows and Leroy Little Bear, two of Canada's leading Aboriginal scholars and teachers, if this rate holds steady, in fifty to seventy-five years there will be no status Indians left in Canada. We'll still have the treaties and we'll still have treaty land held in trust for status Indians by the government.

We just won't have any Indians.

Legally, that is.

So, as the Ducks would say, what is it about us that you don't like?

At that cabin in the mountains of New Zealand, Paul spent the first morning showing me how to bake bread in a pot over an open fire, how to dress a deer haunch, how to sharpen a knife on a river stone. Useful stuff for a life in the woods. Paul was disappointed to discover that I didn't know how to track or read signs, but he reckoned that Indians raised in cities lose those skills.

Don't worry, he told me, in a year or so, you'll be as good as me.

For the next four days, I followed Paul around, watched him set up on a deer trail, watched him shoot deer, watched him cut off their tails so he would have proof that he was doing his job. On the morning of the fifth day, he sent me off on my own.

Make yourself useful, he said. Shoot as many of 'em as you can.

That morning I shot my first deer. That afternoon I packed up my stuff and left Paul a note.

Thanks, it said.

Then I hiked the eight miles out to the trailhead and caught a ride north with a trucker.

So what is it about us you don't like?

You're probably thinking racism is the answer.

Maybe.

Certainly part of it is racism. Not the same brand of racism that created apartheid in South Africa or slavery and segregation in the United States. It's a kinder racism that is cut with a genuine fondness for Natives and Native culture, a racism infused with a suffocating paternalism that can gently strangle the life out of a people. To be sure, it is an affection that is most times misplaced, an affection that is focused on the more exotic, erotic, mysterious, and spiritual aspects of Native life, but it is, nonetheless, an appreciation that is deeply felt and maintained.

So if it's not racism per se, maybe you don't like us because we control large tracts of land and valuable resources, or maybe it's because we get government subsidies and "special" privileges. But none of these should present a serious problem. Corporations own land. They own resources. They get government grants and subsidies. It's one of the benefits of a free-market economy, where the facade of capitalism is supported by public largesse. Matter of fact, if it weren't for the infusion of free public money into the private sector, capitalism would have a very difficult time maintaining itself. Just ask Air Canada or Bombardier or any of the major players in the Alberta oil industry.

Of course, we don't call it "free money." We refer to these public generosities as tax incentives, without mentioning that the incentive is not to create a better society but to make a profit.

Even the fact that Indian land is, by and large, unavailable to the general public shouldn't bother us much. Private hunting clubs own land that no one but club members can hunt on. Fishing clubs own stretches of river that are off-limits to the hoi polloi. Timber companies own vast stands of trees that no one but the company itself can harvest. Drive to the Augusta National Golf Club in Augusta, Georgia, any day of the week and try to play a round of golf. If you're not a member, you can't tee up. Or drive to any one of the gated communities in North America and try to explain to the guard on duty that you just want to look around.

We understand the philosophy of ownership. We believe in the sanctity of property rights. We relish the mystique of exclusivity.

So just think of Indians as a business or an institution or a country club.

If it helps.

But, of course, it doesn't.

I didn't leave deer culling because I was afraid that Paul was right about the world, that things either had value or they didn't. And I didn't leave because I understood that if you believed in such a world, there would be no end to the killing.

Though I should have.

I left because there was no point in my staying. Killing one deer was more than enough, and having done it once, I could not imagine doing it again.

What is it about us you don't like?

Maybe the answer to the question is simply that you don't think we deserve the things we have. You don't think we've worked for them. You don't think we've earned them. You think that all we did was to sign our names to some prehistoric treaty, and, ever since, we've been living in a semi-uncomfortable welfare state of trust land and periodic benefits. Maybe you believe we're lazy/drunk/belligerent/stupid. Unable to look after our own affairs. Maybe you think all we want to do is conjure up the past and crawl into it.

People used to think these things, you know, and they used to say them out loud. Now they don't. Now they just think them.

But if we are successful in that middle-class or upper-middle-class way, if we are able to, as middle North America likes to say, make something of ourselves, and here you can find any number of good Canadian examples — John Kim Bell, Tomson Highway, Dr. Marlene Brant Castellano, Tom Jackson, Nellie Cournoyea, Douglas Cardinal, Mavis Callihoo, Dorothy Grant, Robbie Robertson, Maxine Noel, Daphne Odjig, Graham Greene, Susan Aglukark . . . me — then you tell us we're a credit to our race, the implication being that the rest of our people are not. Or you divide us up into categories where those of us who have not been successful in that peculiar way that North America measures success are seen as authentic, while those of us who have become doctors and educators and artists and politicians and entrepreneurs are dismissed as counterfeit.

What is it about us that you don't like?

Let's look at the matter from a different angle. Why is the government concerned about defining who is an Indian and who is not? There's not an Italian Act that defines who is and who is not an Italian. Or a Russian Act. Or a Greek act. Mind you, in California, in the nineteenth century for a while, Mexicans were legally defined as "White," while Chinese were legally defined as "Indians." But even with the French in Quebec, who occupy much the same position in Canada as Native people do, there has been no legislative effort to distinguish between French and non-French. No French Act.

Yet, like Indians, the French float in a sea of English influence. They control an entire province, a larger land base and more resources than any of the tribes in all of North America. They seem to annoy the English as much as, if not more than, do Native people. And they have to deal with the attitude of many in this country who believe that the special rights the French enjoy — a distinct language, a distinct society — are benefits that, like Native rights, are unearned and undeserved.

The French, I'm sure, feel that they constantly have to reaffirm their right to exist, but they don't have to deal with laws that try to get rid of them. There are no legal divisions for status French and non-status French, the concept of the pure laine being a social construct, not a legal one. Consequently if a French woman marries an English man and her children marry Italians and Greeks and their children marry Australians and Germans and maybe even Indians, they don't, by law, lose their claim to being French.

The only obvious difference between the French and the Indians is that the French represent a formidable voting block, which can decide who comes to power and who does not.

Ah, there's the rub.

And because there's no legal distinction, the French can go on creating more French no matter whom they marry. All they have to do is maintain their language and culture, and they will never lose status, while Indians can disappear even with their languages and cultures intact.

So is the right of identity simply a privilege of power?

Unlike most other ethnic groups, we have two identities, a cultural identity and a legal identity, and the argument that I want to make is that we should be able to take both of them with us wherever we go, whatever we do, and with whomever we do it. For the reality of identity legislation has not simply been to erase Indians from the political map of North America, it has also had the unforgivable consequence of setting Native against Native, destroying our ability and desire to associate with each other. This has been the true tragedy, the creation of legal categories that have made us our own enemy.

When Bill c-31 was passed, for instance, a number of band councils sought to deny members of their own nation — Indians who had reacquired status through the legislation — membership in the band out of fear that the influx of C-31 Indians would drain the tribe's limited resources. And because they did not want to share with people they considered to be outsiders.

As soon as Bill C-31 was passed, it was challenged by three Alberta bands — the Sawridge First Nation, the Tsuu T'ina First Nation, and the Ermineskin First Nation — who insisted that the bands, and not bureaucrats in Ottawa, should be able to set their memberships. "It's not just where do you draw the line," Catherine Twinn, legal counsel for the bands, insisted, "but who draws the line."[4] A valid enough argument as long as you ignore the troublesome echoes of Merrill E. Gates and his "intelligently selfish" Indians.

The bands argued that their objection to Bill C-31 was neither racist nor sexist, that they had no objection to non-status people regaining status, only to the proposition that status and band membership were the same thing and that bands no longer had the legal right to control that membership.

The eight-month-long court case that followed was a montage of the horrors that legislative racism, judicial arrogance, and Native xenophobia can create. The government, which had originally stripped Indians of status, blithely gave it back with little regard to the potential consequences. The judge in the case characterized Indians as primitive and adolescent, in need of governmental control, and argued that oral-history testimony was unreliable and at odds with the authentic, written, historical record that had been created by non-Indians. And the bands, in an unsightly display of fear and loathing, suggested that accepting back into membership people who, for various reasons, legal and personal, had neither lived on the reserve nor been part of the community could have disastrous consequences, including the possibility that the reinstated Indians could band together and vote to liquidate band assets and sell the land.

An ugly thing from all angles.

No doubt there is some clever cretin somewhere who will make the argument that termination legislation is, in fact, the answer to the Indian problem, that once every last legal Indian has been terminated/enfranchised/ vanished, and once every reserve/reservation has been surveyed and sold, Indians will no longer have to deal with the barriers that status has created.

No more Ducks.

But then who will sing for us? Who will dance for us? Who will remind us of our relationship to the earth?

Who will tell our stories?

The one about Coyote and the Ducks, for instance.

Take it. It's yours. Do with it what you will. Tell it to your children. Turn it into a play. Forget it. But don't say in the years to come that you would have lived your life differently if only you had heard this story.

You've heard it now.

AFTERWORDS

PRIVATE STORIES

THE TRUTH ABOUT STORIES is that that's all we are.

The Nigerian storyteller Ben Okri says that "In a fractured age, when cynicism is god, here is a possible heresy: we live by stories, we also live in them. One way or another we are living the stories planted in us early or along the way, or we are also living the stories we planted — knowingly or unknowingly — in ourselves. We live stories that either give our lives meaning or negate it with meaninglessness. If we change the stories we live by, quite possibly we change our lives."[1]

For Native storytellers, there is generally a proper place and time to tell a story. Some stories can be told any time. Some are only told in the winter when snow is on the ground or during certain ceremonies or at specific moments in a season. Others can only be told by particular individuals or families. So when Native stories began appearing in print, concern arose that the context in which these stories had existed was in danger of being destroyed and the stories themselves were being compromised. The printed word, after all, once set on a page, has no master, no voice, no sense of time or place.

Of course, written stories can be performed orally; although, apart from authors on reading tours to promote their books and parents reading to children, this seldom happens.

And oral stories can be stuck in a book.

But for the most part, I think of oral stories as public stories and written stories as private stories. I know I will generate disagreement on this point. After all, we are surrounded by books that can be read by anyone. We have public libraries, public bookstores. There would appear to be nothing private about Shakespeare or Jane Austen or Gabriel Garcia Marquez or Margaret Atwood. These writers and their works are known to the world. But the act of reading is a private act. And no matter how many people may have read a book or an article or a poem or a short story, each person reads that story themselves, by themselves, whereas oral stories generally have an audience in which there is a group dynamic. Though it could be argued that both reading and listening, in the end, are individual acts.

And then there's television.

So I'm probably wrong.

Nevertheless, it's a distinction I make. Oral stories. Written stories. Public stories. Private stories. Stories I can tell out loud. Stories I cannot.

This is one of my private stories.

It is doubtful I will ever perform it as an oral piece because, for a variety of reasons, I choose not to do so.

And because I can't.

This is the only place you will find it. Contained within these mute marks on a silent page.

Sounds portentous, doesn't it. Or at least poignant. Mute marks. Silent page. Hyperbolic language to entice you to read the next sentence. Just another cheap literary trick.

There's a family I know. A family with whom I used to be friends. John and Amy Cardinal and their three children, Franklin, Amos, and Samantha, or Sam as everyone knows her. John is a painter. Amy teaches psychology at a university. Two cars. Two cats. A solid brick home built in the 1920s with hardwood floors and a nice backyard.

Your more-money-than-average Canadian family.

Franklin and Amos are the Cardinals' natural children. Sam is adopted. This is a distinction I am loath to make. Within Native culture, by and large, where a child comes from, and how she becomes a member of a family or a community, is not an issue. I make it here only because I don't want you to think poorly of Amy Cardinal.

Sam suffers from fetal alcohol spectrum disorder (FASD).

For those of you who don't know what fetal alcohol spectrum disorder is, here's a quick tour. Alcohol consumed at any point during a pregnancy can affect the fetus. No amount is known to be safe, any may be destructive to varying degrees. FASD is the designation for a range of neurological disorders that affect the brain as well as other structures. Drinking on or around day twenty-eight, for example, can produce distinctive facial morphology — small, wide-set eye sockets, the absence of a philtrum, a thin upper lip. While not all FASD children exhibit these features, they do share — to varying degrees — an inability to do abstract reasoning, to control impulses, to generalize from one situation to another, to learn from experience, to make choices, and to understand the effect that behaviour has on others.

School is difficult for a child with FASD, and, as she progresses, the workload can become completely and utterly overwhelming. Most often the frustrations that arise from not being able to meet the demands and expectations of others are brought back to the family, and the frustrations are taken out on parents and other siblings. FASD children are extremely difficult to parent under the best circumstances, and there is little chance that they will ever be able to live as completely independent adults.

While you can modify the child's environment and reduce the occasion of stress, there is absolutely nothing you can do to reverse the effects or undo the condition. It is both devastating and completely preventable. It simply requires that women who become pregnant don't drink.

I know. Yet another burden to place on women. Another stone's weight of blame.

This is why I want you to know that Sam's condition wasn't Amy's fault. And I want you to know that it wasn't Sam's fault. And if we wanted to blame someone and could discover who the "bad" mother was, it wouldn't make a bit of difference. Much too late for blame to do any good, much as we love to point fingers. Much too late for blame to make a difference.

We live in a strange world, do we not? We know that alcohol and tobacco are highly addictive drugs, yet we allow their use as part of our ongoing social activities. We encourage companies to ferment a variety of liquors and manufacture cigarettes and cigars of every shape and size, chewing tobacco and snuff. We make few objections to corporate suggestions that drinking and smoking are pleasurable, that these products will help you to be accepted. Even loved.

At the same time, because we understand alcohol and tobacco and their potential for disaster, we maintain boundaries around these highly profitable drugs. Loose ones to be sure. We don't say that you can't smoke or that you can't drink, we just put age limits on these activities and try to regulate where and when you can do them.

You can't smoke in public buildings; do it outside.

You can't drink and drive a car; call a taxi.

But with other drugs such as heroin and crack cocaine, we have no such understanding. These are banned addictive drugs even though they have much the same effects as alcohol and tobacco.

Sanctioned Addictive Drugs and Banned Addictive Drugs.

And the only real difference between them are the stories we tell.

The stories we tell about alcohol are romances. Wine is for lovers, single-malt scotch for successful entrepreneurs, beer for young nubile women and virile young men who can't afford anything else.

The stories we tell about cigarettes are action adventures.

We smoke to look cool, to let the world know that we don't care. Screw you, we say, when we light up. You don't like it? Tough. You want a piece of me? Come and get it.

No one *tells* me what to do.

No one tells *me* what to do.

No one tells me what to do.

When I was younger, we drank beer to feel good and smoked to look good. We drove up and down the main streets of North America, with a six-pack on the seat next to us in case we ran into a good time and our smokes rolled up in the sleeves of our T-shirts so you could see our muscles.

Sanctioned Addictive Drugs. Banned Addictive Drugs.

But great stories. Very effective. Very enticing. Very hard to resist.

It would be simplistic to say that Sam's birth mother must have liked the story about alcohol, for there were probably other stories that she "liked" just as well — the one about being poor, for example, or the one about being worthless — but for Sam and her parents, the story was neither a romance nor an action adventure.

I know what you want to read next. You want to read how Amy and John dedicated their lives to helping Sam, how Family and Children's Services supported the Cardinals and provided them with assistance in coping with Sam's behaviour, how the school Sam went to set up a special program to help her succeed, how the health care community in the town where the Cardinals lived did research on FASD and discovered a methodology, a regimen of vitamins and exercises and special learning aids, perhaps, that allowed Sam to manage her condition, how the Cardinals' friends and neighbours came together, how the community helped to raise this troubled child.

What you want to read is how the distress of a child and a family engaged the compassionate and ethical responses for which North America is supposed to be famous.

Yeah.

That's a story I'd like to read, too.

Unfortunately, North America has no such ethics.

Really we don't. Now, I'm not saying that we don't have *any* ethics. I'm just suggesting that we don't have the ones we think we have.

For example, in North America, we talk about our environmental ethic. And we point to instances such as the *Exxon Valdez* oil spill in Alaska that devastated miles of coastline and the response of the public to that disaster — when hundreds, perhaps thousands, of people rushed in with mops and sponges and began cleaning seabirds, while crews with high-powered steam units blasted the oil off rocks, and boats with oil-retardant chemicals and oil-containing booms surrounded the spill and sucked it up — as proof that such an ethic exists. Certainly the outcry over the offence was loud and sustained.

And then there was Enron.

Remember that one? Business ethics. When it was discovered that the company's directors had cooked the books, that they had lied about Enron's economic health to make the stock's position in the market look much better than it was, that they had made substantial profits just prior to the collapse by selling off their personal holdings, investors and the public stood ready to lynch everyone involved in the scandal.

To listen to the noise generated by these two events, you would have thought that we cared.

But, in fact, we don't. Not in any ethical way.

Oh, sure, we don't like oil on our beaches, and we don't like to be robbed. In this day and age, oil tankers, we insist, are supposed to be safe. Financial institutions are supposed to be bastions of integrity.

But we do nothing to prevent such disasters from happening again. And if they do (as they most certainly will), our reaction will be the same, because the story we tell about moments such as these is that they shouldn't have happened, that they're someone else's fault, that they're the price we pay for our way of life, that there's no way to avoid them completely, that the environment and investor confidence will recover eventually.

John and I were friends. Good friends. We went out for coffee at least once a week, caught the occasional action film, played a little golf, told jokes, talked. We went to

Barbados together with our families and to Costa Rica, shared a cottage at Lake Simcoe, flew to British Columbia and skied Panorama. My kids played with his kids. I knew that Sam's behaviour was a problem, but when she was around other people and had things to keep her occupied, she managed reasonably well. There would be flare-ups, to be sure, moments when everything came to a stop while we sorted out emotions.

And, of course, I expected that, as time went on and as Sam matured, the difficulties would work themselves out.

But they didn't. By the time Sam was a teenager, the behavioural problems had intensified. I told John that all teenagers go through difficult periods, that eventually they come out the other side as reasonable human beings. It was a platitude, something you say because it's what you're supposed to say, not because it's true, and both of us knew it.

John did not manage any of this very well. He was angry much of the time. Angry that Sam was the way she was, angry that Amy had insisted on adopting because she had wanted a daughter, angry because he felt trapped in a world not of his making, angry that they couldn't get any meaningful help from health professionals.

Angry that he was angry.

For my part, I began to keep my distance. I stopped calling. I made excuses. I didn't return his calls. Not all at once. Gradually. Until it was as though we had never known each other.

Then one day, I decided I should call and see how he

was doing. Amy answered the phone. In the background, I could hear Sam abusing her mother, calling her a bitch and slamming doors. At one point Sam grabbed the phone and yelled "Fuck off" into the receiver. After that I listened to Amy's breathing, while Sam raged through the house, the sound of breakage trailing in her wake.

Is this a bad time? I asked.

No, Amy told me, no problem.

I felt guilty. Maybe John hadn't exaggerated the situation. I had been his friend, and I had done nothing to help.

Is John around? I asked.

No, said Amy. He's not here anymore.

A number of years ago, the Canadian government closed down the cod industry on the East Coast. It was, in many ways, a futile gesture. The cod were already gone, had been going for years. The reason was simple. Overfishing. The government knew about the potential problem long before it became a problem. So did the fishers. Yet when the fishery wound up on death's doorstep, everyone seemed surprised, shocked, angry that such a thing had happened. The fishers blamed the government, the government blamed the fishers, everyone blamed the large offshore foreign trawlers as well as seals, global warming, El Niño, Native people, the decline of religion, illegal immigrants, and homosexuality.

Could such a thing have been prevented?

Of course.

Okay, so why didn't we prevent it?

The oil industry and our oil-based economy, not just in Canada but in the world, depend on two things for their continued existence. The ability of geologists to find new fields of oil and our willingness to ignore the obvious, that, at some point, we're going to run out of oil. This would suggest that reducing energy consumption, curbing the proliferation of private cars and multilane highways, and converting to sustainable and reliable sources of energy such as solar, tidal surge, or wind power would be our first priorities. In fact, we have no such priorities. We have only the hope that the exhaustion of the oil supply will not happen in our lifetime.

It's not that we don't care about ethics or ethical behaviour. It's not that we don't care about the environment, about society, about morality. It's just that we care more about our comfort and the things that make us comfortable — property, prestige, power, appearance, safety. And the things that insulate us from the vicissitudes of life. Money, for instance.

Money is wonderful insulation. The more money you have, the higher the R-value. It won't buy you happiness, but it will keep out the chill of poverty. It won't provide you with complete privacy, but it will keep the neighbours and the social workers at bay.

One of my sweet dreams is to be able to buy a piece of property on the ocean with a panorama of the coastline and the mountains. Lot number six at Rosie Bay in Tofino. I'd build a modest cedar-plank house with nine-foot coffered ceilings, hardwood floors, double-hung windows with muntins, and a terrific kitchen — Sub-Zero refrigerator, six-burner Aga gas stove, Miele dishwasher, dark granite countertops.

Maybe a modest koi pond just off the deck.

Oh, and a tile shower enclosure in the master bedroom with etched-glass doors, multiple heads, and pewter vents near the floor to let in steam.

I have a cartoon on the wall next to my computer. It shows a wagon train of pioneer frogs in the middle of a desert. They look around the endless waste of sand and cactus and one frog says to the other, "We'll put the swamp here."

Insulation. And comfort.

I know. It's an easy job to be critical, easy enough to look around the world, easy enough to find bad behaviours everywhere, easy to say that the proof of what we truly believe lies in what we do and not in what we say.

So I'll say it.

Perhaps we shouldn't be displeased with the "environmental ethics" we have or the "business ethics" or the "political ethics" or any of the myriad of other codes of conduct suggested by our actions. After all, we've created them. We've created the stories that allow them to exist and flourish. They didn't come out of nowhere. They didn't arrive from another planet.

Want a different ethic? Tell a different story.

We could tell ourselves stories about community and co-operation. We do that, you know. From time to time. Every so often, we hear a good disaster story — families caught out by a flood, a town levelled by an earthquake, whales beaching themselves — and we respond with a ferocity and moral resolve that does us proud.

A lost little girl in the forest will get us off our couches as quickly as a fire in the kitchen.

I was in Oklahoma City a few years back and stopped by the site of the federal building that Timothy McVeigh bombed to rubble. The people of Oklahoma City have turned it into a memorial, complete with a reflection pool, a grassy area, and a series of lighted glass chairs, one for every person killed in the blast. On the west side of the memorial is a run of cyclone fencing on which people have hung cards and photographs and words of sympathy, inspiration, and condolence. Here and there, teddy bears have been stuffed into the wire in memory of the children who had been in the daycare when the bomb exploded.

So perhaps I'm wrong. Perhaps we do have the kind of ethics we imagine we have. Maybe they're just not steady. Not dependable. Ethics of the moment. Potential ethics. Ethics we can draw on when we feel the need to do so. Ethics that can be wrapped in newspaper and stored in the freezer. Seasonal ethics.

Annuals rather than perennials.

About six months ago, I ran into John on the golf course where we used to play. He was pleased to see me, he said, as we relaxed in the clubhouse, as happy as he deserved to be. The boys were managing well. Amy was coping with Sam. At least she didn't have to deal with his anger anymore.

They're better off without me, he said. Leaving was the best thing I could have done.

He didn't accuse me of deserting him, of not helping. And I didn't apologize for not being there when he and Amy could have used my help. Not help, perhaps. Sympathy. Comfort. Understanding. Just being there.

Would it have made a difference?

This is the question we always ask *after* we have given up.

I don't tell this story out loud because it's not much of a story. No plot. No neat ending. No clever turns of phrase. And because I always end up weeping. Not for John and Amy. Not for Sam's brothers. And not for Sam.

But for myself.

And for the world I've helped to create. A world in which I allow my intelligence and goodwill to be constantly subverted by my pursuit of comfort and pleasure. And because knowing all of this, it is doubtful that given a second chance to make amends for my despicable behaviour, I would do anything different, for I find it easier to tell myself the story of my failure as a friend, as a human being, than to have to live the story of making the sustained effort to help.

So you can see, the story about John and Amy Cardinal is not a story I want to tell. It is, quite probably, a story that I should not tell. It is certainly not a story that I want anyone to hear.

I could have made this up, you know. A sad story to play on your sympathies. An anecdote to give my concerns a human face.

I didn't.

But you've no reason to trust me when I say that I know John's story as well as I know my own.

After all, I'm a storyteller.

You can have it if you want. John's story, that is. Do with it what you will. I'd just as soon you forget it, or, at least, not mention my name if you tell it to friends. Just don't say in the years to come that you would have lived *your* life differently if only you had heard this story.

You've heard it now.

NOTES

Chapter 1: "You'll Never Believe What Happened" Is Always a Great Way to Start

1. Jeannette Armstrong, in *Speaking for the Generations: Native Writers on Writing*, ed. Simon Ortiz (Tucson: University of Arizona Press, 1998), 181.
2. Leslie Silko, *Ceremony* (New York: Viking Press, 1977), 138.
3. Basil Johnston, "How Do We Learn Language?" in *Talking on the Page: Editing Aboriginal Oral Texts*, eds. Laura Murray and Keren Rice (Toronto: University of Toronto Press, 1999), 14.
4. Linda McQuaig, *All You Can Eat: Greed, Lust and the New Capitalism* (Toronto: Viking, 2001), 12.

Chapter 2: You're Not the Indian I Had in Mind

1. Laura Coltelli, *Winged Words: American Indian Writers Speak* (Lincoln: University of Nebraska Press, 1990), 156.

2. Louis Owens, *I Hear the Train: Reflections, Inventions, Refractions* (Norman: University of Oklahoma Press, 2001), 91–92.

3. Owens, 103.

Chapter 3: Let Me Entertain You

1. Andrea Menard, "The Halfbreed Blues," *Prairie Fire* 22, no. 3 (autumn 2001): 32.

2. Samuel Eliot Morison, *The European Discovery of America: The Southern Voyages*, 1492–1616 (Oxford: Oxford University Press, 1974), 65.

3. William Brooks Greenlee, ed., *The Voyages of Pedro Alvares Cabral to Brasil and India* (London: Hakluyt Society, 1938), 10–11.

4. David B. Quinn, ed., *New American World: America from Concept to Discovery* (New York: Arno, 1979), 1:149.

5. Douglas Edward Leach, *Flintlock and Tomahawk: New England in King Philip's War* (New York: Macmillan, 1958), 22.

6. Leach, 22.

7. Charles H. Lincoln, ed., *Narrative of the Indian Wars*, 1675–1699 (New York: Charles Scribner's Sons, 1913), 89.

8. Benjamin Trumbull, *A Complete History of Connecticut*, 1797 rpt. (New York: Arno, 1972), 1:80.

9. John Richardson, *Wau-Nan-Gee, or, The Massacre at Chicago: A Romance of the American Revolution* (New York: H. Long and Brother, 1852), 100.

10. J. Franklin Jameson, ed., *Narratives of New Netherlands* (New York: Barnes and Noble, 1967), 126.

11. Philip Deloria, *Playing Indian* (New Haven: Yale University Press, 1998), 25.

12. John Heckeweller, *Account of the History, Manners, and*

Customs of the Indian Nations Who Once Inhabited Pennsylvania and the Neighboring States (Philadelphia, 1818), 25.

13. Robert F. Berkhofer Jr., *The White Man's Indian* (New York: Vintage, 1979), 89.

14. Loring Benson Priest, *Uncle Sam's Stepchildren: The Reformation of United States Indian Policy, 1865–1887* (Norman: University of Oklahoma Press, 1979), 137.

15. Michael Paul Rogin, *Fathers and Children: Andrew Jackson and the Subjugation of the American Indian* (New York: Alfred Knopf, 1975), 216.

16. Charles Eastman, *From the Deep Woods to Civilization* (Lincoln: University of Nebraska Press, 1977), 193.

17. Eastman, 195.

18. John Stackhouse, "Comic Heroes or 'Red Niggers'?" *Globe and Mail*, November 9, 2001.

19. Stackhouse.

20. Stackhouse.

Chapter 4: A Million Porcupines Crying in the Dark

1. Leslie Silko, *Ceremony* (New York: Viking Press, 1997), 2.

2. Louis Owens, *I Hear the Train: Reflections, Inventions, Refractions* (Norman: University of Oklahoma Press, 2001), 20.

3. Owens, 27.

4. N. Scott Momaday, *House Made of Dawn* (New York: Harper & Row, 1968), 95–96.

5. James Fenimore Cooper, *The Deerslayer* (New York: New American Library, 1963), 50.

6. Cooper, 50.

7. Cooper, 41.

8. Cooper, 116.

9.   Momaday, 103–104.
10. Beth Brant, "Recovery and Transformation: The Blue Heron," in *Bridges of Power*, eds. Rose Brewer and Lisa Albrecht (Gabiola, B.C.: New Society Publishing, 1990), 119.
11. Robert Alexie, *Porcupines and China Dolls* (Toronto: Stoddart, 2002), 5.
12. Alexie, 12.

Chapter 5: What Is It About Us That You Don't Like?

1.   Diane Glancy, *The West Pole* (Minneapolis: University of Minnesota Press, 1997), 70.
2.   Arrell Morgan Gibson, *The American Indian: Prehistory to the Present* (Norman: University of Oklahoma Press, 1980), 494.
3.   J. Leslie and R. Maquire, eds., *The Historical Development of the Indian Act*, 2nd ed. (Ottawa: Treaties and Historical Research Centre, Indian Affairs and Northern Development, 1978), 115.
4.   Catherine Twinn, in Windspeaker [website], "Classroom Edition Topic: Bill c-31" [cited August 7, 2003], available from http://www.ammsa.com/classroom/CLASS1C-31.html.

Afterwords: Private Stories

1.   Ben Okri, *A Way of Being Free* (London: Phoenix House, 1997), 46.

The CBC Massey Lectures Series

The Universe Within
Neil Turok
978-1-77089-015-2 (p)

Winter
Adam Gopnik
978-0-88784-974-9 (p)

Player One
Douglas Coupland
978-0-88784-972-5 (p)

The Wayfinders
Wade Davis
978-0-88784-842-1 (p)

Payback
Margaret Atwood
978-0-88784-810-0 (p)

More Lost Massey Lectures
Bernie Lucht, ed.
978-0-88784-801-8 (p)

The City of Words
Alberto Manguel
978-0-88784-763-9 (p)

The Lost Massey Lectures
Bernie Lucht, ed.
978-0-88784-217-7 (p)

The Ethical Imagination
Margaret Somerville
978-0-88784-747-9 (p)

Race Against Time
Stephen Lewis
978-0-88784-753-0 (p)

A Short History of Progress
Ronald Wright
978-0-88784-706-6 (p)

The Truth About Stories
Thomas King
978-0-88784-696-0 (p)

Beyond Fate
Margaret Visser
978-0-88784-679-3 (p)

The Cult of Efficiency
Janice Gross Stein
978-0-88784-678-6 (p)

The Rights Revolution
Michael Ignatieff
978-0-88784-762-2 (p)

The Triumph of Narrative
Robert Fulford
978-0-88784-645-8 (p)

Becoming Human
Jean Vanier
978-0-88784-809-4 (p)

The Elsewhere Community
Hugh Kenner
978-0-88784-607-6 (p)

The Unconscious Civilization
John Ralston Saul
978-0-88784-731-8 (p)

On the Eve of the Millennium
Conor Cruise O'Brien
978-0-88784-559-8 (p)

Democracy on Trial
Jean Bethke Elshtain
978-0-88784-545-1 (p)

Twenty-First Century Capitalism
Robert Heilbroner
978-0-88784-534-5 (p)

The Malaise of Modernity
Charles Taylor
978-0-88784-520-8 (p)

Biology as Ideology
R. C. Lewontin
978-0-88784-518-5 (p)

The Real World of Technology
Ursula Franklin
978-0-88784-636-6 (p)

Necessary Illusions
Noam Chomsky
978-0-88784-574-1 (p)

Compassion and Solidarity
Gregory Baum
978-0-88784-532-1 (p)

Prisons We Choose to Live Inside
Doris Lessing
978-0-88784-521-5 (p)

Latin America
Carlos Fuentes
978-0-88784-665-6 (p)

Nostalgia for the Absolute
George Steiner
978-0-88784-594-9 (p)

Designing Freedom
Stafford Beer
978-0-88784-547-5 (p)

The Politics of the Family
R. D. Laing
978-0-88784-546-8 (p)

The Real World of Democracy
C. B. Macpherson
978-0-88784-530-7 (p)

The Educated Imagination
Northrop Frye
978-0-88784-598-7 (p)

Available in fine bookstores and at www.houseofanansi.com